To

Kerry,

KIDs
Now They Come
With a Manual

Matt Hudson & Paul Dearlove

You know You know
this stuff!

love
Matt & P x

Kids Now They Come with a Manual. Copyright © 2014. All rights reserved. No part of this publication may be reproduced, distributed, or transmitted in any form or by any means, including photocopying, recording, or other electronic or mechanical methods, without the prior written permission of the publisher, except in the case of brief quotations embodied in critical reviews and certain other noncommercial uses permitted by copyright law. For permission requests, write to the publisher, addressed "Attention: Permissions Coordinator," at the address below.

Authors: Matt Hudson and Paul Dearlove
Designer: Karl Adams (GetMediaWise.com).

Permission:
Matt Hudson (matt@matthudson.com)
3 Park Villas,
The Green,
Wallsend
Newcastle upon Tyne
Tyne and wear
England,
NE28 7NW

ISBN-10: 1502380129
ISBN-13: 978-1502380128

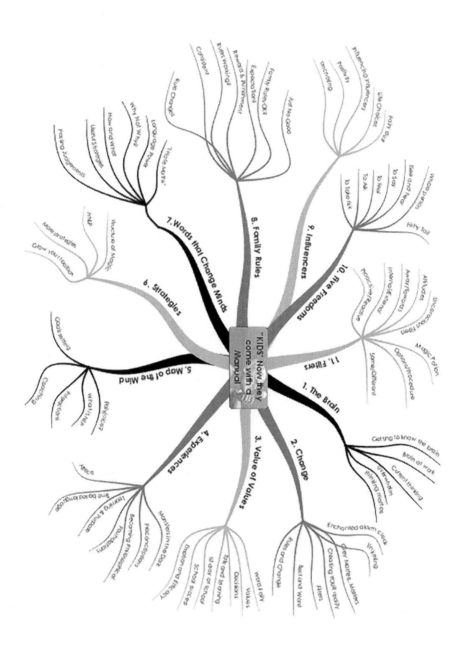

"KIDS' Now, they come with a Manual?

1. The Brain
- Getting to know the brain
- Brain at work
- Gr-amotram
- Current thinking
- Thinking matrix

2. Change
- Enchanted alarm clock
- Investing
- Obey, Master, Master
- Choosing YOUR reality
- Filters
- Feet and Want
- Rules and Change

3. Value of Values
- Values
- Decisions
- 1st day at school
- School success
- 7 trusten on the ligt
- Monsters in the dark
- Becoming Principled,
  foundations
- Learning & Purpose
- Atitia

4. Experiences
- Time based language

5. Map of the Mind
- Particulars
- What is it on
- Influences
- Coaching
- Clock and hat

6. Strategies
- Structure of Magic
- HNP
- More strategies
- Grow your Feedback

7. Words that Change Minds
- Triple Mats'
- Language Power
- Why Not What
- Used Strengths
- How and What
- passing Judgements

8. Family Rules
- Consistent
- Rule Change
- Rules Working?
- Reward & Punishment
- Expectations
- Family Rules OK?
- Just No Good

9. Influencers
- Influencing Influencers
- Follow it
- anchoring
- Life Choices
- Fairy tale
- Whole person
  - Raise and level
  - To feel
  - To do
  - To say
  - To ask
  - To take risk

10. Five Freedoms

11. Filters
- Self/Other
- Sameness/Difference
  - Away/Towards
  - Internal/External
  - proactive/Reactive
  - Art Values
  - Options/Procedure
  - Magic Pill on

Contents

Acknowledgements

Matt Hudson: Thank you to our young clients, who made the magic happen, the parents and teachers who trusted us with their precious youngsters and the many students who attend our trainings. You inspire us and encourage us to continue to find better ways of communicating.

Thank you to Henk and Carla Beljaars who now have their book Coach with Inzigd translated into English. Your friendship means a lot to us as we forge ahead helping people in the UK and The Netherlands spreading the word!

Thank you, Kim Cowie for your continual support and going through the first drafts, and thank you to our secret Facebook page, who guided the format of this, final edition. My friends and colleagues Tom Brennan, Michael Shane, Anne Railton, Karl Adams and Shirley Ann Gaut.

A special thank you to my Wife Sonya and sons Alan, Karl and Kurtis, you are the wind beneath my wings.

Paul Dearlove: Thank you to the few teachers in our own schooling who believed we could. All colleagues and young people at Bewerley Park and Vesbaek who nurtured my adventurous spirit, comrades at NRAIS who helped me to grow, and P4C gurus, Roger, James and Will who inspired me to question.

Lynn, Amy, Ruth, Sophie and Bump who remind me why I'm here and to Matt and Sonya for their continuing friendship, wisdom and energy… long may it grow!

And an extra special thank you to our editor, JD van Zyl, without whom this book would have appeared very different. Together we can make happy kids and happier families

Foreword

Children: we love them. Sometimes we understand them but often we don't. We try to raise them the best we can. As parents, mentors, caregivers, guides, awakeners and also as teachers.

We meet children in all kinds of places, all ages, in good and in bad situations or somewhere in between. We spend hours helping them to grow into the beautiful people they will be and who they in essence already are. Every now and then, we wonder why habits or patterns emerge as they do and how we might encourage change for the better instead of for the worse.

In this book, Matt and Paul describe ordinary situations and possible solutions. They don't start from a judgmental kind of perspective. They rather discuss it in pure honesty. There is no need to hide it or lie about the questions we have; we all encounter them in our lives. The authors acknowledge that we need to encounter these situations in order to grow and learn. And so do children. We can all learn and grow if we choose to.

This book hands you some theoretical perspectives about change, experiences, brain development, communication, language and patterns, and accompanies these concepts with practical applications. From several starting points the book discusses the various roles we can adopt to help children to grow. Tips and tricks, dos and don'ts. It is all about how to get to know our children better. But moreover, it is about getting a better understanding of who we are as parents, why we do the things we do and why we react the way we do.

We want children to feel good because we know that if they feel good, they learn more and do better. We want them to prosper, to feel the ebb and flow of life and to grow a little bit more every day. We want to look inside their eyes and discover the colours of their soul. We want to actually discover who they truly are and to support them to be themselves wherever they are.

Freedom is a treasure that resides in our heart. When we are open and honest we are able to share that freedom with the children we meet. Only then can we help them to stay as creative as they are, naturally and profoundly. By doing that, we help them to grow into resilient, sentient beings, aware of themselves and the world around them with a learned sense of responsibility. And we can help them to pursue their dreams. How? By being responsible and creative ourselves, by learning and growing each day of our lives and by modeling these attitudes and behaviours for them.

This book helps us to start or even continue doing that. And it reminds us of the beautiful fact that every day is a brand new day—filled with possibilities to grow. Let's start from there, with a flexible, creative and persistent mindset and keep on learning.

Dr. Cyrille A.C. van Bragt
Director MLE Fontys University for Child Education
The Netherlands

Introduction

"The intuitive mind is a sacred gift and the rational mind is a faithful servant. We have created a society that honours the servant and has forgotten the gift."

Albert Einstein

This book aims to parallel Einstein's thoughts. We have compiled sound, solid and rational communication strategies for the servant, and then woven intuitive, inspirational and aspirational client stories to remind you of the gift.

With this in mind your child can:
- learn more efficiently
- process information quicker
- become more resilient
- perform better on tests
- engage in productive dialogue
- have the ability to see multiple "right" answers
- integrate socially and make friends easier

At the same time we are seeking to teach through metaphors and client stories from our personal experience, because this is such an ancient way of transmitting multiple meanings, cultural values, ethics and morality. The use of pronouns like he/she are used interchangeably throughout the book, and the same with singular child and plural children, parent, caregivers, mother and father. The reader should adjust these to their own unique situation.

Logic can be easily dismissed as right or wrong by the listener, rather like taking aim at a battle ship and firing a torpedo in order that you may be able to sink the problem; only to find, after you have pushed the button, that the vessel has radar and averts your incursion with unerring accuracy.

On the other hand, a story that is well placed, fun and intriguing, woven through with humour and curiosities will glide effortlessly towards the target, gently scratch its hull, leaving the ocean to breach the previously untouchable craft with new learning and connections. Or perhaps you might consider why sink a perfectly seaworthy means of conveying thoughts when colluding with the crew may entice the captain to change its course.

With this in mind, we would encourage you to turn your head away from the land you know and invite you to travel with us to discover new shores.

The Fairy God Mother
(And the street that disappeared)

Once upon a time, there was a little boy who was alone in the schoolyard, after his first day at school. There were, of course, lots and lots of other children whose parents had come to collect them, but this little lad had been forgotten—or he thought. As the throng of people meandered through the school gates, the child tagged along close behind, unnoticed by the excited gaggle of mums and their children who were busy clucking about how exciting their first day had been.

As the walk continued, the group became smaller and smaller, as fragments of the brood headed into their homes. As the last pair faded into a cul-de-sac, the four year old thought to himself, "It can't be far now," and valiantly marched onwards along the busy main road.

He couldn't remember the name of his street; he had never needed to know it before now. He could remember that at one end there was a fast food chip shop, so that would make it easier for him to spot.

What our lone ranger didn't know was that the "chip shop" in question was part of a chain and they all looked the same, a bit like McDonalds does today.

So, when the faint smell of chips began guiding him by the nose, to another chip shop that was part of the chain, he stopped, he sat down on the step and he puzzled over this next challenge.

After a while there appeared a lady who worked in the chip shop. She came out and asked the boy if she could help him. The boy's eyes welled up with salt water,

"I can't go home," he whimpered. *"Why not?"* asked the inquisitive lady.

"Because, I've been to school today and come back and someone has 'pinched' (stolen) my street," he sniffled.

The lady smiled, hugged the child and bringing him into the warmth of the shop, she said, *"I'll find your street for you".*

The little boy had been very fortunate because this was no ordinary lady. She was his Fairy God Mother and sure enough, within no time at all, a policeman arrived to show the boy where his "pinched" street had been found.

The boy's mother and father had been frantically searching for hours, and desperately praying for the safe return of their son, who had managed to wander out of one of two school gates. His poor mother was distraught, as the desperate minutes turned into hours without her baby. Needless to say they were overjoyed to see him, alive and well.

Life would soon take on a new school routine, but the boy would never forget the good fairy and he would visit her and her family many times as the years went by. No one would ever know that she was enchanted except for the boy who kept their secret.

The lady in the chip shop was called Mrs. Tomlinson, and that boy is now sitting here and writing these words to you. She found me, Matt, when I didn't even know I was lost. This book is to help parents to be magical and to help the child in all of us to find our way home.

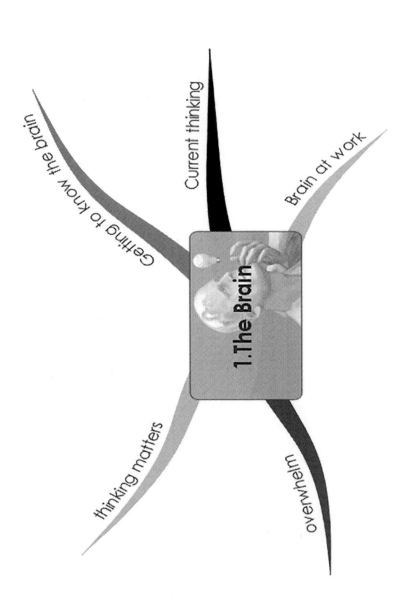

Chapter 1
The Brain

"The human brain has 100 billion neurons, each neuron connected to 10 thousand other neurons. Sitting on your shoulders is the most complicated object in the known universe."

Michio Kaku

In order for us to help our children, it makes sense to first look at the brain and its many complex functions. Don't worry! We aren't about to baffle you with science, just make some simple observations about how things that happen on the outside can impact on the inside. And how that can ultimately lead to patterns of behaviour and responses to certain situations or stimuli that become fixed for years and years, or at least until new information comes along to overwrite the old data.

The brain—it is the organ we can't live without, yet the one we can't seem to understand either. It is a part of our anatomy that we really do want to understand and use to the best of its abilities—but it remains a mystery at best. An enigma might be a better way to describe the brain.

It's the organ that controls it all:

- Breathing
- Muscle function
- Movement
- Thoughts
- Pain sensations
- Everything we do

But what is it about how the brain that helps us to learn and grow? That is an interesting question.

Getting to Know the Brain

The brain is a biological miracle, an extremely sophisticated and complex piece of equipment that shares some of the characteristics of a house pet. This is an animal that wants to do things that make you happy, but sometimes just gets overwhelmed by all of the things it could do and all of the possibilities out there.

So, you need to learn how to educate it, in much the same way that there are specific approaches that get results when training a puppy.

Sure, you can work on yelling at the brain and the person with the brain, hoping they will just "get" what you're trying to tell them, but that's probably not going to give you the results you want.

In the same vein, you may have tried using a louder voice with your child, but that didn't seem to help. Why? Because the brain isn't as simple as an on-and-off switch. You don't turn an animal on or off. First, you need to learn how they think and then you need to figure out what the best way would be to work with the way they think.

The truth of the matter is that we all think differently and we all think about things based on how we've thought in the past and based on our previous experiences. For example, if you thought that the stove wasn't hot because you touched it without burning yourself, but then you touch it once and it hurts, you learn quickly to incorporate that new information into your wealth of knowledge.

Just one simple lesson can give you the opportunity to find out more about your world and how it works. From there, you might learn that you need to slowly touch things in order to find out if they're hot or not. And you might learn that while things might not look hot, they might in fact be scorching.

So knowledge works much like a cascade of lessons; it isn't just one single lesson about stoves being hot. But that's not all that your brain can do and that's not all your brain is doing for you.

"No one asks how to motivate a baby," behavioural psychologist B. F. Skinner wrote in *Walden Two*. "A baby naturally explores everything it can get at, unless restraining forces have already been at work. And this tendency doesn't die out, it's wiped out."

A Brain at Work

The pre-frontal cortex is the part of the brain that acts as a trainer for your brain. It's the part of your brain that receives all of the information that you find on a daily basis, decides where to send it, and then moves onto the next bit of information.

This is a lot for it to do, and when the brain is overwhelmed by new information, it's really no wonder that a kid can feel overwhelmed. Today, in the world of instant information that comes from multiple directions, your child is constantly taking in information, without necessarily having a good way to organise it and then use it. A child doesn't yet have the sophisticated mental filing cabinet in place that you have developed over decades.

Phew. Just thinking about that is tiring.
The brain is getting "orders" from various different sources, in the same way a pet might. Those sources include:

- Mum and dad
- Friends
- Siblings
- Teachers
- The Internet
- Television
- Books
- Magazines
- Videogames, etc.

A child's brain is filled up with new "commands", and it doesn't seem able to process all of them at once. What it does is to simply collect the information and use it as best it can.

Along the way, some of the information will be tossed to the side since their grey matter doesn't know how to use it. Other bits of information will be used immediately and then forgotten. By aiming to give your kids experiential learning you will be helping them to retain and process information far easier.

We are emotional beings, after all, and are system is highly sensitive to this.

This "training" of the brain does not have to be such a confusing task. You can help your child begin to learn how to organise all of the incoming information so that it's not only easier to use and to remember, but so that they can actually apply the knowledge they have in their brain to future projects and questions.

And that's where learning begins.

The Brain's Overwhelm: A Case Study

Johnny is twelve years old and he's already getting overwhelmed by the homework he has to do. Not only does he have to work on math, but he also has science homework, an English reading assignment and an extra credit history assignment.

He looks at his homework list and he doesn't know where to start, so he thinks about starting with the things that are the shortest. He thinks that since he can get those done quickly, the rest will have more time to be finished before bed.

But the easy ones are so easy that he takes his time on them, and they take twice as long as they ought to have. Before he knows it, it's already been two hours and he still has the tough assignments to go.

His brain is switching back and forth between rugby, hockey trials next week and the detention he still has to tell his mum about. And another thirty minutes pass by. Johnny decides that he should start his next homework assignment, which then leads him to feel nervous about finishing it.

He picks up his video game and starts to play, promising himself that he would only play until his character died. But Johnny gets on a roll and makes it through seven levels without any troubles.

He looks at the clock and realises that he can't finish his homework that night. So he decides that he should just forget about the rest and hope that he can get up early to do some of it. Or maybe he'll just talk to his teacher again about getting more time to do it.

This is a common situation for many kids, even though they might not want it to be one. They don't want to be the one who has trouble finishing their homework, but with all of the things they have to do, it's harder than ever to get ahead and to stay focused.

Some parents, caregivers and teachers might think this is sheer laziness, but it's really a question of not having the tools to understand how to finish their homework effectively, even if they are distracted.

Getting rid of those distractions will be helpful, but how do they get started? That's where you can come in to help.

How We Think Matters

When you think, you don't give it a second thought, of course. But you might begin to see how the way you think isn't helping you at work, in life or in learning.

When you have a child, you can see how the patterns they learn now will influence the way in which they act the rest of their lives. You don't have to let it be this way. You can do more for them than you might have had done for you.

And when this happens, you can begin to change their lives. A child who can think more clearly and more effectively will:
- Do well in school
- Manage their time wisely
- Be more effective at home
- Be ready for life's challenges
- Be ready for more difficult tasks

A child who is ready for more than they are handling right now is a child who is better prepared.

While the brain might be organised to work in one way, this doesn't mean you can't change the way a child thinks, no matter who they are and no matter how they have learned and processed information in the past. By learning to process information in new ways, the brain can handle a lot more. So how do we ensure that our children remain learners?

According to Stanford University psychologist Carol Dweck, a global authority on achievement and success, mindset matters. If you are reading this book one may imagine that you have a belief that intelligence is a malleable quality, a potential that can be developed. On the other hand, your experience with your kids might lead you to believe that intelligence is a fixed trait based on your innate talent and abilities. Where do you fit in? And more importantly, which mindset is likely to get the best results from your children? A quick look at the table below will give you a fair indication about where you fit in on Dweck's continuum.

Growth	Fixed
1. Learn, Learn, Learn	**1.** Look intelligent at all costs
2. Work smart, effort is the key	**2.** It should come naturally
3. Capitalise on mistakes	**3.** Hide mistakes
4. It's much more important for me to learn things in my classes than it is to get the best grades	**4.** The main thing I want, when I do my schoolwork, is to show how good I am at it!

A **growth** mindset allows learners to:
- Embrace learning and growth
- Understand the role of effort in talent creation
- Maintain confidence and effectiveness in the face of challenges and setbacks.

The characteristics of a teacher, parent, caregiver or mentor with a growth mindset are:
- Portrays skills as acquirable
- Values passion, effort and improvement over natural talent
- Presents themselves as mentor/collaborator, not judge.

Dweck's work suggests that having a fixed mindset provides no recipe for recovery from a setback. She also suggests our mindsets determine the language we use which in turn tells students what we believe and what we value.

Dweck's research looked at the difference in results achieved between three groups. The first group received what she called intelligence praise like, "Wow, that's a good score. You must be smart at this." The second received effort or process praise, such as, "Wow, that's a good score. You must have worked really hard". A third control group just got, "Wow, that's a good score".

Which group do you think went on to engage willingly with further hard challenges? And which group or groups were reluctant to engage with further challenges especially after "failing"?

So what do we praise?
The answer according to Dweck is: effort, struggle, persistence despite setbacks, strategies, choices and choosing difficult tasks, learning and improving.

To foster a growth mindset, what are you going to do differently? The first step could be to check out www.brainology.us and obtain a copy of Carol Dweck's book.

Learning goals inspire a different chain of thoughts and behaviours than *performance goals*. Students for whom performance is paramount want to look smart even if it means not learning a thing in the process. For them, each task is a challenge to their self-image, and each set back becomes a personal threat. So they pursue only activities at which they are sure to shine and avoid the sorts of experiences that will enable them to grow and flourish in any endeavour.

Students with 'learning goals', on the other hand, take necessary risks and don't worry about failure because each mistake becomes a chance to learn. People with performance goals think intelligence is fixed from birth. People with learning goals have a growth mindset about intelligence, believing it can be developed.

To use Johnny's situation, he is currently operating from the fixed mindset. He sees his homework as difficult and doesn't think that he will be able to demonstrate his intelligence to the level he feels he should be able to. It should come naturally, like playing his videogame, but it doesn't. By ignoring the rest of his homework and playing the game he gets to feel that he is good at something. However, he is really lying to himself as he wastes valuable learning time creating many excuses to not complete the task.

Whereas, if Johnny uses a growth mindset he would be able to see all of his homework as learning, working smarter with his time and mental approach to the task. If he gets anything wrong he benefits by learning from this and adjusting for next time.

A special gift

When you sign up to our mailing list at matthudson.com you will receive a free handbook, which is full of useful games and exercises for you and your young ones.

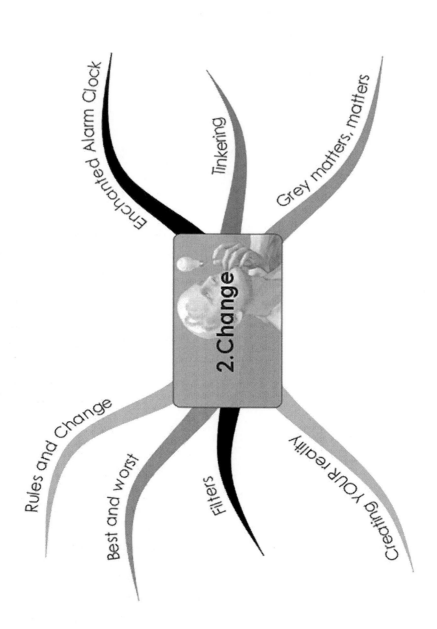

Enchanted Alarm Clock

Tinkering

Grey matters, matters

2.Change

Rules and Change

Best and worst

Filters

Creating YOUR reality

Chapter 2
Dealing with Change
"If you change the way you look at things, the things you look at change."

Wayne Dyer

An Enchanted Alarm Clock

One of the challenges we all face as a child is the ability to wake up in a dry bed. Nowadays there is an ever-greater urgency to have our children take control of their bladders earlier, so they can be farmed out to pre-school and then into the world. There are however many children who for one reason or another just can't seem to manage to make it through the night without the inevitable puddle. Doctors and specialists recommend no liquids after a certain time and even medication; but the fact is, your child can manage to control their bladder, all by themselves. They may just need a little help in succeeding. Below are two examples; the first is Matt's and the other is from the late great psychiatrist Milton Erickson, and it's brilliant.

When children come to me with this problem I ask them how it is that they know it's time to go to the toilet during the day. Invariably, I get them to realise that they have a feeling and it is that feeling which causes them to go to the toilet. But, when they are sleeping, comfortably in their bed, fast asleep, the feeling isn't any good, because nothing feels nicer than being snuggled in your own dry bed. Then I ask them what wakes them up in the morning? Usually it's one of their parents telling them it's time to get up or some noise or other. "Now, this is the key!" I tell them excitedly. Inside your mind you have an enchanted alarm clock that can talk to your bladder so when it's almost full the magical clock rings and wakes you up. That way you can begin to have a dry bed more and more…

Erickson began by explaining to the child that he couldn't help her, as he was just like all of the other doctors who had failed to help her. "But you already know something but you don't know that you know it. As soon as you find out what it is that you already know and don't know that you know, you can begin having a dry bed." Then Erickson told her, "I am going to ask you a very simple question and I want a very simple answer.

Now, here's the question: If you were sitting in the bathroom, urinating, and a strange man poked his head in the doorway, what would you do?"
"I'd freeze!"
"That's right. You'd freeze—and stop urinating. Now, you know what you already knew, but didn't know that you already knew it. Namely, that you can stop urinating at any time for any stimulus you choose. You really don't need a strange man poking his head in the bathroom. Just the idea of it is enough.

You'll stop. You'll freeze. And when he goes away you will start urinating.

"Now, having a dry bed is a very difficult job. You might have your first dry bed in two weeks. And there has to be a lot of practice, starting and stopping.

That's all right. Your body will be good to you. It will always give you further opportunities to start and stop. It would surprise me very much if you had a permanently dry bed within three months. It would also surprise me if you didn't have a permanently dry bed within six months.

And the first dry bed will be much easier than two dry beds in succession. And three dry beds in succession is much harder. And four dry beds in succession is still harder. After that is gets easier. You can have five, six, seven, a whole week of dry beds. And then you can know that you can have one week of dry beds and another week of dry beds."[1]

Tinkering With Pre-programming

When a computer is shipped to you, it already comes with a certain number of settings as predetermined by the factory. The brain works in the same way.

When your kid (Knowledge Integration Device) is born, he/she will have a certain way that his/her brain functions, allowing them to process information in a certain way.

But as with your computer, when you learn more about how it works, you can begin to tinker with the settings. You can work with the settings and apply them to how your life works. You can put the folders on your desktop in a certain arrangement, for example, or you can make sure that when information comes into your life, you use it in a certain way.

Or you might change the way that information is presented so it is easier to integrate. You don't want to simply throw all of the information you store on your computer into one folder. That wouldn't be helpful. Just imagine trying to dig the photos out from your summer holiday in France four years ago if everything on your PC has been dumped into one folder – it would be a nightmare!

Similarly, you don't want your children to have a tough time coping with the knowledge and information they receive. It's time to learn how the default settings work in the brain... and then to start learning how to adjust them.

The Grey Matter Matters

The brain is receiving information every second of the day. It is also processing information at the same time, so it's constantly working to learn something or to take something new in or to connect the new with the already known.
Say you have a new piece of information that you just learned.

This piece of information can be used in one of three ways:
1. be used instantly
2. be forgotten
3. be stored for later use

While this sounds simplistic, if you think about the last time you had to learn something for a test or for an event in your life, you'll see that you followed this exact approach.

Say you learned that two plus two was four. If you were adding things up at that exact moment, then you could use that information instantly. If you weren't interested in the information at that moment, you might have nodded and then forgotten it. But if you knew that you needed to use that information at a later stage, like in an exam, then you might retain that information in your brain.

The brain wants to use the information it finds, but it sometimes needs help to retain it, especially when it isn't clear at the moment how the knowledge would be used later on.

Creating Your "Reality"

When you or your child receives information, there are three steps that take place to help you make sense of it all and to store the information in the best way:

1. Observing the event

When information happens in the world, we observe it through a variety of different senses:
- We touch it
- We taste it
- We listen to it
- We see it
- We smell it

Of course we are even consciously aware that we are going through these steps, they happen completely naturally and afterwards our brain digests the information to form a complete picture.

For example, when a child goes to the aquarium for the first time and they reach into the touch tank where they see a starfish for the first time – they want to put it into their mouth, smell it and crumple their nose at the fishiness of it.

2. Filtering the event

Once you have observed an event, it passes through a whole lot of filters that determine what will stick – a little like a kid who only likes blue M&Ms and who tosses any other colour to the side. Depending on our beliefs, values, and fears, there are different filters that can be used:[2]
- generalising
- deleting
- distortion

We can choose to generalise the event and interpret it as just another similar event. For example, if Susan hears about a math test, she might assume it's going to be difficult because another test was difficult.

Or she can delete the information. Let's say she wants to pursue a career as a fashion stylist and knows she won't need math and as a result she thinks it isn't important, then she will simply delete it from her consciousness.

And if the math test is something that worries Susan, she might begin to distort its reality in her life. She might begin to think it's the most important test ever, which can cause her to completely freak and break out in spots, which create a different experience of the test in the moment.

According to Naom Chomski, filters are the brain's way of beginning to handle information.[3] They may not be grounded in reality, but they certainly create our reality.

3. Making a map of the event

Once you have filtered certain information you start to make different pictures of the information in your brain.

You might use these different tools for representing information in your brain:
- Pictures
- Sounds
- Feelings
- Smells
- Tastes
- Code words

All of these tools are helpful for storing the information, though they might not always be completely true to reality. If you are able to change the way you and your kids filter information, then your internal "map" will be more effective and helpful.

Your "map" influences your internal state

When you create an internal map of what you've learned, you will begin to perceive the world in a different light. In the same way that if you study a map of the New York subway you will have a very different perception of the Big Apple than if you study an over-ground map of its biggest tourist sites.

Remember that math exam? If Susan were to think the exam was the hardest test ever, this might influence her to study harder in order to pass. She might talk about the test as something that she needs to "fight" in order to "win".

The way she has stored the information will impact the way that she will react and interact in the world. If she changes the way she filters information, or you change the way your child filters information, then you both can change the way you store information, and also the way you react to the world.

When a thought enters...

Every time a thought enters your child's head, their brain wants to deal with it in a certain way by sending it to one of two main destinations (even if they aren't even aware of that process happening).

Waking up to your thinking

Every moment, your brain is processing millions of pieces of information—in every single moment. The numbers are infinitely greater than we can imagine as every day neuroscience is making new discoveries. It is thought that more electrical impulses are generated in one day by a single human brain than by all the telephones in the world, and the slowest any information passes from one neuron to another is 260mph. It is a truly phenomenal piece of equipment.

But with all of that capacity it is easy for our brains to get itself into a bit of a tizzy, as it tries to decide what it needs to act on and what it doesn't need to worry about. All on its own.
In truth, we're all perpetually distracted so we're consciously unconscious of the thoughts in our brains. We are always processing information, but we're just not thinking about thinking until it is suggested to us that we do so.

Like right now, because you are more engaged and you are thinking specifically about thinking, you're picking up on more thinking than you might have ever done before.

And by doing that, you bring more consciousness to thinking, which in turn allows you to do just that—even more thinking!

How Filters Work

When your brain processes information, you need to have a way to streamline what you do and do not take in. If you were to take in all of the billions of bits of information around you every single second of every single day, you would completely frazzle your brain.

The filtering system of your mind allows you to hang onto the bits of information you need while also allowing you to avoid the pieces of information you don't really need. A little bit like a water filter that blocks impurities so that you end up with a glass of beautiful crystal clear drinking water. Everyone wins.

Delete

When you take in information, even though you don't realise it, you filter things immediately. Fancy putting that to the test? Before you read any further take 30 seconds and look around the room you are in for everything that is blue.

It can be any shade of blue. Then close your eyes and recall all the blue items you saw. I am sure you can recall a great many. Now, close your eyes and recall everything you saw that was green. Nowhere near as many? Chances are you might not have noticed anything that is green, because you had your "blue filter" on while scanning the room. Your mind works exactly the same way.

If you need to find a certain book on a shelf, for example, you might "delete" information you don't deem to be important, like every other book on the shelf that isn't the book you need. You might begin by deleting the books that you know to be bigger than the book you need, then the bookshelf that you know doesn't include that book, etc.

You delete information because you don't need it at that point in time, not because it's not important. In a different context, the same data might be essential and then you might reprioritise everything to align with this. See how that works?

Distort

One of the things that can get us into trouble is the way that we distort information that we take in. Now, this sounds like you're taking in information and making it different from what it is, but this isn't necessarily a bad thing.

For example, if you were to have the belief that the sky was red and someone else has the opinion that the sky is blue, you both feel you are right. You might each see the sky as the different colours you believe it to be.

So, you argue with the other person about what you see versus what they see. You both think you're right and you might both think the other person is wrong.

When you distort information, it's as though you're saying that there is certain information that is right to you, you distort your own sense of reality. You might think something completely different from what another person says because you truly believe what you believe.

There's nothing inherently wrong with this process, as everyone has their own experience of reality, based on what they have experienced before and based on what they feel to be true and what they feel to be false. But when you begin to say that only your experience is right, that's when things can get a little stickier.

And that's when people argue about what they believe. The way you distort things in your mind will change the way you feel things are or aren't, and that in turn is based on the information you receive from the world around you.

Generalise

Finally, when you take in new information, you might generalise that information, based on what you have experienced in the past—this is when words like "always" and "never" come into play. The brain believes that if you hurt your hand when you touched a hot kettle in the past, all kettles will do the same thing. So, you might decide to be more careful when you're around kettles.

When a trainer trains an elephant, from the time they are young, they are tied with a rope to a nail in the ground. If the elephant is young when they start training, they truly believe that the rope and the nail in the ground are holding them in place.

They try to pull on the rope and they can't get free. The elephant learns to generalise their experience. They feel that since they are in the same position, they will not be able to get free of the rope, even as they get bigger and weigh more.

The generalisation of their beliefs causes the elephant to always feel they are captive when they are tied to the nail with the rope.

When we have certain experiences in life, we generalise them because that's how things make more sense to us. We believe that each experience teaches us something about the future. And often, we don't try to look outside of that experience.

Keeping these filters in mind when it comes to kids allows you to see that children process information in the same way that adults do, but since they have a limited set of experiences, it seems that children will have different outcomes for their thinking than adults do.

By learning that experience can impact how a person feels in the future, this also shows parents that the more positive experiences a child has, the more that will influence their thinking and behaviour in the future.

What's The Best That Can Happen?

Clinical psychologist Martin Seligman did research into the idea of positive psychology as a notion about ten years ago.[4] The field analyzes areas like happiness, satisfaction, and hope. Another psychologist, Barbara Fredrickson who has spent her career studying positive emotions, describes in her recent book, *Positivity*, how a positive outlook in life will release creativity, improve ability to enjoy the world's pleasures, and increase contentment with your life and relationships.[5]

Fredrickson identifies a three-to-one ratio of positive to negative emotions as the key to maximum success. She lists ten forms of positivity, they are: joy, gratitude, serenity, interest, hope, pride, amusement, inspiration, awe and love. Additionally, Fredrickson offers a place online for you to test your own positivity: www.PositivityRatio.com.

Here are some core messages about positivity:
- Positivity changes your future
- Positivity feels good
- Positivity transforms how your mind works
- Positivity impacts greatly on negativity
- Positivity obeys a tipping point
- Positivity can increase by following her guidelines

Does that mean that to live a happy and fulfilled life all you have to do is sit in the garden, repeat a mantra and make sure your thoughts are positive? Not quite. But we'll get to that.

What's The Worst That Can Happen?

Journalist and author Oliver Burkeman recently wrote in The New York Times: "What if all this positivity is part of the problem? What if we're trying too hard to think positive and might do better to reconsider our relationship to 'negative' emotions and situations?"[6]

Burkeman cites research by the psychologist Gabrielle Oettingen and her colleagues about how visualising a successful outcome, under certain conditions, can make people less likely to achieve it.[7] She rendered her experimental participants dehydrated, then asked some of them to picture a refreshing glass of water.

The water-visualisers experienced a marked decline in energy levels, compared with those participants who engaged in negative or neutral fantasies. Imagining their goal seemed to deprive the water-visualisers of their get-up-and-go, as if they'd already achieved their objective.

What about affirmations? Those cheery statements intended to lift the user's mood by repeating them: "I am a lovable person!" "My life is filled with joy!" Psychologists at the University of Waterloo concluded that such statements make people with low self-esteem feel worse—not least because telling yourself you're lovable is liable to provoke the grouchy internal counterargument that, really, you're not.

Even goal setting, the ubiquitous motivational technique of managers everywhere, isn't an undisputed boon. Fixating too vigorously on goals can distort an organisation's overall mission in a desperate effort to meet some overly narrow target, and research by several business-school professors suggests that employees consumed with goals are likelier to cut ethical corners.

Though much of this research is new, the essential insight isn't. Ancient philosophers and spiritual teachers understood the need to balance the positive with the negative, optimism with pessimism, a striving for success and security with an openness to failure and uncertainty.[8] The Stoics, a school of Greek philosophers from the Third century, recommended "the premeditation of evils," or deliberately visualising the worst-case scenario:

"Get rid of the judgment, get rid of the 'I am hurt', you are rid of the hurt itself"

- Marcus Aurelius[9]

This tends to reduce anxiety about the future: when you soberly picture how badly things could go in reality, you usually conclude that you could cope.

Besides, they noted, imagining that you might lose the relationships and possessions you currently enjoy increases your gratitude for having them now. Positive thinking, by contrast, always leans into the future, ignoring present pleasures.

Buddhist meditation, too, is arguably all about learning to resist the urge to think positively—to let emotions and sensations arise and pass, regardless of their content according to Burkeman.

"From this perspective, the relentless cheer of positive thinking begins to seem less like an expression of joy and more like a stressful effort to stamp out any trace of negativity. A positive thinker can never relax, lest an awareness of sadness or failure creep in. And telling yourself that everything must work out is poor preparation for those times when they don't. You can try, if you insist, to follow the famous self-help advice to eliminate the word "failure" from your vocabulary—but then you'll just have an inadequate vocabulary when failure strikes.

The social critic Barbara Ehrenreich has persuasively argued that the all-positive approach, with its rejection of the possibility of failure, helped bring on our present financial crises.[10] The psychological evidence, backed by ancient wisdom, certainly suggests that it is not the recipe for success that it purports to be. To sum up then, we need a bit of both: Upside thinking and down side thinking.

How We Change Our Brain

Our brain is not static and it does not necessarily want to remain the same. Because the brain is designed to take in new pieces of information, it makes sense that it is designed to change.

Each time a person learns something new, a wonderful thing happens: the brain physically changes. The structure of the brain will adjust slightly to accommodate the new way of thinking.

New connections form in the brain, new synapses are created, and old neural networks can be rerouted. Yes, the brain is a magical tool and we don't even know the half of it yet. In the last ten years we have learned more about the brain than in the previous millennium.

John Medina, a developmental molecular biologist who has a lifelong fascination with how the brain deals with and organises information, offers 12 principles in his book Brain Rules.[11] These rules are aimed at helping people survive and thrive at work, home and school. They are:

Rule 1: Exercise boosts brainpower

- Our brains were built for walking – 12 miles a day!
- To improve your thinking skills, move
- Exercise gets blood to your brain, bringing it glucose for energy and oxygen to soak up the toxic electrons that are left over
- It also stimulates the protein that keeps neurons connecting
- Aerobic exercise just twice a week halves your risk of dementia

Rule 2: Survival – The human brain also evolved

- We don't have one brain in our head – we have three. We started with a "lizard brain" to keep us breathing. We then added a brain like a cat's, and then topped those with the thin layer of Jell-O known as the cortex – the third, and powerful, "human" brain
- We took over the Earth by becoming adaptable to change, coming down from the trees to the savannah when the climate changed
- Going from four legs to two to walk on the savannah freed up energy to develop a complex brain
- Symbolic reasoning – the ability to perceive one thing as another – is a uniquely human talent. It may have arisen from our need to understand one another's intentions and motivations, allowing us to coordinate within a group

Rule 3: Wiring – Every brain is wired differently

- What you do and learn in life physically changes what your brain looks like – it literally rewires it
- The various regions of the brain develop at different rates in different people
- No two people's brains store the same information in the same way in the same place
- We have a great number of ways of being intelligent, many of which don't show up on IQ tests

Rule 4: Attention – We don't pay attention to boring things

- The brain's attention "spotlight" can focus on only one thing at a time – no multitasking
- We are better at seeing patterns and abstracting the meaning of an event than we are at recording detail
- Emotional arousal helps the brain learn
- Audiences check out after 10 minutes, but you can keep grabbing them back by telling narratives or creating events rich in emotion

Rule 5: Short-term memory – Repeat to remember

- The brain has many types of memory systems. One type follows four stages of processing: encoding, storing, retrieving, and forgetting
- Information coming into your brain is immediately split into fragments that are sent to different regions of the cortex for storage
- Most of the events that predict whether something learned will also be remembered occur in the first few seconds of learning. The more elaborately we encode a

memory during its initial moments, the stronger it will be
- You can improve your chances of remembering something if you reproduce the environment in which you first put it into your brain

Rule 6: Long-term memory – Remember to repeat

- Most memories disappear within minutes, but those that survive the fragile period strengthen with time
- Long-term memories are formed in a two-way conversation between the hippocampus and the cortex, until the hippocampus breaks the connection and the memory is fixed in the cortex – which can take years
- Our brains give us only an approximate view of reality, because they mix new knowledge with past memories and store them together as one
- The way to make long-term memory more reliable is to incorporate new information gradually and repeat it in timed intervals

Rule 7: Sleep – Sleep well, think well

- The brain is in a constant state of tension between cells and chemicals that try to put you to sleep and cells and chemicals that try to keep you awake
- The neurons of your brain show vigorous rhythmical activity when you're asleep – perhaps replaying what you learned that day
- People vary in how much sleep they need and when they prefer to get it, but the biological drive for an afternoon nap is universal
- Loss of sleep hurts attention, executive function, working memory, mood, quantitative skills, logical reasoning, and even motor dexterity

Rule 8: Stress – Stressed brains don't learn the same way

- Your body's defense system – the release of adrenaline and cortisol – is built for an immediate response to a serious but passing danger, such as a saber-toothed tiger. Chronic stress, such as hostility at home, dangerously deregulates a system built only to deal with short-term responses
- Under chronic stress, adrenaline creates scars in your blood vessels that can cause a heart attack or stroke, and cortisol damages the cells of the hippocampus, crippling your ability to learn and remember
- Individually, the worst kind of stress is the feeling that you have no control over the problem – that you're helpless
- Emotional stress has huge impacts across society, on children's ability to learn in school and on employees' productivity at work

Rule 9: Sensory integration – Stimulate more of the senses

- We absorb information about an event through our senses, translate it into electrical signals (some for sight, others from sound, etc.), disperse those signals to separate parts of the brain and then reconstruct what happened, eventually perceiving the event as a whole
- The brain seems to rely partly on past experience in deciding how to combine these signals, so two people can perceive the same event very differently
- Our senses evolved to work together – vision influencing hearing, for example – that means that we learn best if we stimulate several senses at once
- Smells have an unusual power to bring back memories, maybe because smell signals bypass the thalamus and head straight to their destinations, which include that

supervisor of emotions known as the amygdala

Rule 10: Vision – Vision trumps all other senses

- Vision is by far our most dominant sense, taking up half of our brain's resources
- What we see is only what our brain tells us we see, and it's not 100% accurate
- The visual analysis we do has many steps. The retina assembles photons into little movie-like streams of information. The visual cortex processes these streams, some areas registering motion, others registering colour and so on. Finally, we combine that information back together so we can see
- We learn and remember best through pictures, not through written or spoken words

Rule 11: Gender – Male and female brains are different

- The X chromosome that males have one of and females have two of – though one acts as a backup – is a cognitive "hot spot," carrying an unusually large percentage of genes involved in brain manufacturing
- Women are genetically more complex, because the active X chromosomes in their cells are a genetic mix of Mom and Dad. Men's X chromosomes all come from Mom, and their Y chromosome carries less than 100 genes, compared with about 1,500 for the X chromosome
- Men's and women's brains are different structurally and biochemically –men have a bigger amygdala and produce serotonin faster, for example –but we don't know if those differences have significance
- Men and women respond differently to acute stress:

Women activate the left hemisphere's amygdala and remember the emotional details. Men use the right amygdala and get the gist

Rule 12: Exploration – We are powerful and natural explorers

- The desire to explore never leaves us despite the classrooms and cubicles we are stuffed into. Babies are the model of how we learn—not by passive reaction to the environment but by active testing through observation, hypothesis, experiment, and conclusion. Babies methodically do experiments on objects, for example, to see what they will do.
- Google takes to heart the power of exploration. For 20 percent of their time, employees may go where their mind asks them to go. The proof is in the bottom line: fully 50 percent of new products, including Gmail and Google News, came from "20 percent time".

John Medina has recently published <u>Brain Rules for Baby</u> (2014) and has been generous enough to let us reproduce his top tips for parents with children from 0 to 5 years old. Find John Medina at <u>www.brainrules.net</u>.

His work bridges the gap between what scientists know and what parents practice. Just one of the surprises: The best way to get your children into college? Teach them impulse control. The benefits of applying these rules will save you time, money and more importantly promote a healthier connection between you and your child.

Brain Rules for Pregnancy
Healthy mom, healthy baby

Key points:
- In the first half of pregnancy, babies want to be left alone
- Don't waste your money on products claiming to improve a preborn baby's IQ, temperament, or personality. None of them have been proven to work
- In the second half of pregnancy, babies begin to perceive and process a great deal of sensory information. They can smell the perfume you wear and the garlic on the pizza you just ate
- The mother-to-be can boost baby brain development in four ways: gaining the proper weight, eating a balanced diet, exercising moderately, and reducing stress

Brain Rules for Relationship
Start with empathy

Key points:
- Eight out of 10 couples experience a huge drop in marital quality during the transition to parenthood
- Hostility between parents can harm a newborn's developing brain and nervous system
- Empathy reduces the hostility
- The four most common sources of marital turbulence are: sleep loss, social isolation, unequal distribution of household workload, and depression

Brain Rules for Smart Baby: Seeds
Feeling safe enables learning

Key points:
- There are some aspects of your child's intelligence which you can do nothing about; the genetic contribution is about half of that
- IQ is related to several important childhood outcomes, but it is only one measure of intellectual ability
- Intelligence has many ingredients, including a desire to explore, self-control, creativity, and communication skills

Brain Rules for Smart Baby: Soil
Face time, not screen time

Key points:
- Here's what helps learning: breast-feeding, talking to your children, guided play, and praising effort rather than intelligence
- The brain is more interested in surviving than in getting good grades in school
- Pressuring children to learn a subject before their brains are ready is only harmful
- Activities likely to hurt early learning include overexposure to television, learned helplessness, and being sedentary

Brain Rules for Happy Baby: Seeds
Make new friends but keep the old

Key points:
- The single best predictor of happiness? Having friends
- Children who learn to regulate their emotions have deeper friendships than those who don't.
- No single area of the brain processes all emotions.

Widely distributed neural networks play critical roles.
- Emotions are incredibly important to the brain. They act like Post-it notes, helping the brain identify, filter, and prioritise.
- There may be a genetic component to how happy your child can become.

Brain Rules for Happy Baby: Soil
Labelling emotions calms big feelings

Key points:
- Your infant needs you to watch, listen, and respond
- How parents deal with their toddlers' intense emotions is a huge factor in how happy they will be as adults
- Children are happiest if their parents are demanding and warm
- Emotions should be acknowledged and named but not judged

Brain Rules for Moral Baby
Firm discipline with a warm heart

Key points:
- Your child has an innate sense of right and wrong
- In the brain, regions that process emotions and regions that guide decision-making work together to mediate moral awareness
- Moral behaviour develops over time and requires a particular kind of guidance
- How parents handle rules is key: realistic, clear expectations; consistent, swift consequences for rule violation; and praise for good behaviour
- Children are most likely to internalise moral behaviour if parents explain why a rule and its consequences exist

Brain Rules for Sleepy Baby
Test before you invest

Key points:
- The central fact of newborn sleep is that it is nothing like adult sleep. Newborns only have two speeds: "active sleep" and "quiet sleep". They ride the Tower of Terror
- There is no one-size-fits-all answer for sleep issues
- Do you think baby's wants and needs are the same thing during the first year of life? Or not? It's up to you. Science does not know which one you should choose
- Once baby is 6 months old, choose a plan for better sleep, evaluate your efforts, and then get ready to change your plan.

Experiences colour your reality

Things that happen to and around us also have an impact on the way we experience life and the way we interpret information.

The brain is able to learn once and remember this forever. For example if you burn your finger accidently as a child, you don't need to pop it under a flame fifty years later to see if it still burns, because your brain takes that experience and keeps you safe with it. However, if a dog bites you and you think all dogs are bad then the same process may create a phobic response from that point on, as your brain remembers the dog incident and connects fear to it every time you see a dog.

When you begin to introduce new experiences to your kids, you not only give more information, but you ask them to begin to create a new set of filters based on this new information.

You ask them to consider new information, even if they don't realise it. The more events a child encounters that might have different conditions, the more confused she might become along the way. This is good, as confusion is the step before enlightenment. A child will grow and develop greater thinking skills when allowed to dwell in confusion. The challenge, however, lies with the adult not displaying signs of stress when confusion arises.

In addition, events that seem to have differing consequences can make a kid less likely to trust any situation. Conversely, this might also begin to teach more critical thinking skills as they learn that all information might be interpreted in a new way, depending on the situation. Confused? Good enjoy the feeling of your brain creating new learnings and remember to talk to others about your experience around the event.

Experiences might include:
- Family events
- School events
- Work events
- Friend events
- Traumatic events
- Happy events
- Holidays, etc.

The events in our lives colour who we are and how we process information. We draw and make meanings from these observations, thus creating values.

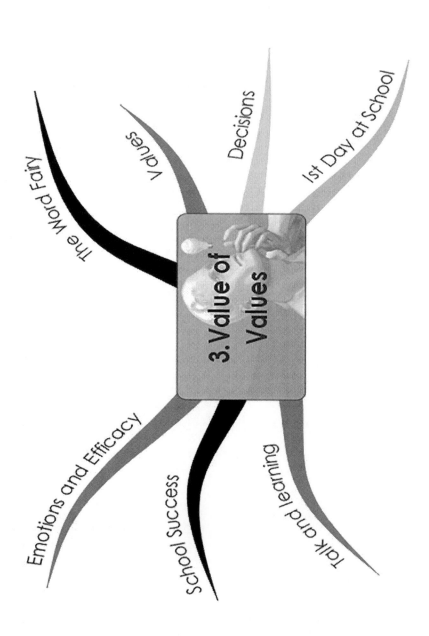

The Word Fairy

Values

Decisions

1st Day at School

3. Value of Values

Emotions and Efficacy

School Success

Talk and learning

Chapter 3
The Value of Values

"When you take the time to actually listen, with humility, to what people have to say, it's amazing what you can learn. Especially if the people who are doing the talking also happen to be children."

Greg Mortenson

Author of 'Stones into Schools: Promoting Peace With Books, Not Bombs, in Afghanistan and Pakistan'

Learning To Read With the Word Fairy

On the last day of school before the Christmas holidays, Matt was picking up his boys as usual and wishing everyone a 'Merry Christmas', when his son's teacher asked to have a quiet word with him. She told him that Kurtis had reading difficulties and would need to have extra support in the New Year in order to catch up. Matt can tell the rest of the tale.

I walked home with a very heavy heart. Over the preceding months whenever my wife Sonya or I attempted to read with Kurtis, he would close down and sulk, so we knew there was a problem. But now, as parents, how were we going to help our son if he wouldn't open up to us?

As we tucked the guys into bed that night, it suddenly struck me: Why not work with Kurt when he is asleep? That way there can be no conscious blocking of information, and at any rate, what's the worst that could happen?

So, I waited until he had been sleeping for about twenty minutes, which was about the right amount of time in accordance with what I could glean from research into

Ultradian Rhythms. My idea was simple—walking into Kurt's room I asked him if he was a sleep and he gave no reply. Next I told him that I was going to hold his hand and talk to him for a little while.

I sat holding his hand and talked to him about fairies and in particular, the Word Fairy, and how she would wander into his mind that night with lots of letters and they would have fun playing together and she would show him new words, so that reading would be becoming easier and easier. The whole piece would take about ten minutes and I repeated the process every night over the following two weeks.

I never made mention of the conversations to Kurtis, during the day, as I didn't want to risk his barriers coming up again. By the end of the holiday period he was reading comics and magazines. He returned to school as a confident reader.

 Kurtis went on to do a lot of theatre and stage performance work and currently sings in his own band and writes his own songs and music.

I have given this technique to many parents and it appears to have great impact on their children, even though the parents aren't hypnotherapists.[12]

Values

Since a child is born with an awareness of right and wrong, it is crucial that you support this development by displaying and discussing the meanings of "values" and their importance. When you look at the word "values", a few things might pop into your mind:

- Beliefs
- Religion
- Power
- Money
- Morals
- Family

You get the idea. When each person thinks about values, or their set of values, a different idea might pop up. While you might think that values are something that cannot be changed or that are only held onto by individuals, this is not the case.

When you are in a family unit, your child is going to be influenced by your values—in one way or another.

For example: James is a hard-working banker who lives in the south of London and usually arrives home after his twin boys, Edward and William, have gone to sleep. Whether he wants it to or not, the twins will be influenced by James' not being at home much. James means well but how will his boys translate this? Work is more important than family? Daddy likes work more than me! I am not as important as money! And so on. There is no end to how a child might internalise this, so the key is to help the child to understand what is happening and its purpose.

If you want to create a strong system of values for your child, you will need to model them and you will need to live by them. When this happens, your child will also use these values as an opportunity to filter out some of the information they hear and see each day.

It might be a good idea to begin to think about the way that you, your partner and your family are expressing your values to your kids. If you have conflicting values, now might be a good time to start thinking about how you can make your values more congruent in terms of the experience your children have at home.

All values aren't equal

Richard Barrett, a global authority on the evolution of human values in business and society, suggests that, "Our values reflect what is important to us. They are a shorthand way of describing our individual and collective motivations. Together with beliefs, they are the causal factors that drive our decision-making."[13] He compares his level of consciousness model with Maslow's hierarchy of needs—that famous pyramid explanation that says only once our basic needs like food, shelter and the likes are met, can we begin to focus on more advanced needs, like relationships and expressing yourself.

The first three levels of consciousness focus on our personal self-interest –satisfying our physiological need for security and safety, our emotional need for love and belonging, and our need to feel good about ourselves through the development of a sense of pride in who we are, and a positive sense of self-esteem.

Abraham Maslow referred to these as "deficiency" needs. We feel no sense of lasting satisfaction from being able to meet these needs, but we feel a sense of anxiety if these needs are not met.

When these needs are paramount in our lives, we are conditioned by the expectations of those around us—by our social environment (the family and the culture we were brought up in). We align, and are loyal to the groups with which we identify.

The focus of the fourth level of consciousness is on transformation—learning how to manage, master or release the subconscious, fear-based beliefs that keep us anchored in the lower levels of consciousness. During this stage of our development, we establish a sense of our own personal authority, and our own voice. We are able to let go of our need to identify with our social environment because we have learned how to master our deficiency needs.

We now choose to live by the values and beliefs that resonate deeply with who we are. We begin the process of self-actualisation by focusing on our individuation.

The upper three levels of consciousness focus on our need to find meaning and purpose in our existence; actualising that meaning by making a difference in the world.

Let's look at a more concise breakdown of Barrett's "Value Centre" based on each level, the focus on that level and the main motivation of each:

- Service: Devoting your life to self-less service in pursuit of your passion or purpose and your vision.
- Making a Difference: Actualising your sense of purpose by cooperating with others for mutual benefit and fulfillment.
- Internal Cohesion: Finding meaning in your life by aligning with your passion or purpose and creating a vision for your future.
- Transformation: Becoming more of who you really are by uncovering your authentic self and aligning your ego with your soul.

Healthy motivations

- Self-esteem: Feeling a sense of personal self-worth
- Relationship: Feeling a sense of love and belonging
- Survival: Feeling secure and safe in the world

Unhealthy motivations

- Low Self-esteem: Underlying anxieties about not being respected and not being enough
- Poor Relationships: Underlying anxieties about not being accepted and not being loved

- Extinction: Underlying anxieties about not being safe or secure and not having enough

In our workbook you can find strategies for drawing forth both personal and family values. Without alignment between these two powerful forces your family and home will be building its future on a foundation of sand. For more information on Barrett's Value Centre, you can go to www.valuescentre.com.

Decisions

"Nothing is more difficult, and therefore more precious, than to be able to decide."
Napoleon Bonaparte

Whenever someone makes a decision, they change the person they are. While the consequences of that decision may not always be positive, the way they think and the way they respond the next time are influenced.

The decisions that your children make and are able to make right now will influence who they are and how they think when the same situation arises later.

So the child who was bitten by a dog can choose between deciding "all dogs are bad", which will create a phobic response, and deciding "that dog was bad". That way she processes specific information attached to that context in that moment. The result? No phobia just new learning.

Depending on how they viewed the decision they made, they might choose to:
- Seek out similar decisions
- Avoid similar decisions
- Learn new ways of handling decisions

When you begin to introduce new ideas to a child and allow them to make new decisions, they begin to see that the world is malleable and that it can be adjusted, depending on how it is reacted to.

The decisions we all make influence who we are and who we intend to become.

Try this short exercise to test your decision making resolve, for best effect answer only one question at a time and cover the rest up:

1. Write down quick notes about how you feel about failure and mistakes.
2. Write down everything you learned to do before the age of 10.
3. Write down everything you have ever learned to do without making a mistake.
4. Write down any successes that wouldn't have happened if you hadn't made a mistake, or if you hadn't "failed" at something.
5. Write down the most important lessons you have learned because of failure or mistakes.
6. Write quick notes about what you feel about failure and mistakes.

"There is one art of which everyman should be master: the art of reflection."

Samuel T Coleridge

Do you Consider Yourself a Learner?

Learners follow a variety of approaches and use different tools, methods and strategies that help them to get more out of life and out of their thinking processes.

Establish values

Since values are an important part of the learning process, you will want to make sure the family values are as clear as possible. This might include having a family meeting to talk about the values of the family and how these values might be used in the everyday world.

Talk about thinking

Yes, you might want to be more cognisant of your own thinking and how it is coloured by your experiences. Not only will this show your kids how to become more aware, but they will find they are more aware as well. Thinking about thinking and talking about thinking is vital.

Work through thoughts

Allow your children to see why you think your thought processes will be helpful to them. You will also want to show them why you make certain decisions. By describing your thought process out loud, you will allow them to be clearer about what goes into thinking and how they might begin to look at their own thoughts.

Model Flexibility

Thinking creatively is a skill and probably the most powerful way for your kids to acquire this ability is by you doing it and talking about it with them. Edward De Bono, the "father of lateral thinking", suggests that in order to encourage and develop creative thinking our thoughts must be challenged in order to produce a new way of being.

"So, let's imagine if we can't do it that way, what is an alternative?" De Bono says. "Sometimes the situation is only a problem because it's looked at in a certain way. Looked at in another way, the right course of action may be so obvious that the problem no longer exists."

Be clear about your motivations

When it comes to helping your children, it's always best to be as clear as possible about why you are doing what you are doing. Be honest that you just want the best for them and that you want to help them. While they might not believe you at first, the more you can be honest with them, the more they will respect your ideas and your input.

Talking about learning

"Of all the tools for cultural and pedagogical intervention in human development and learning, talk is the most pervasive in its use and powerful in its possibilities. Language not only manifests thinking, but also structures it, and speech shapes the higher mental processes necessary for learning"
Robin Alexander (2005 IACEP keynote)[14]

When we talk with kids about their learning, all kinds of areas in the brain light up. Not all talking leads to better thinking. Children need an appreciation of sound, critical and creative patterns of questioning and reasoning. In the beginning you can be the model, a guide on the side so to speak, encouraging dialogue such as "could you explain?" or "can you give me an example?" or "is that always the case?" The best thing you can do is to allow your kids to grow in responsibility themselves.

Encourage them to ask better questions and reassure them that developing arguments and making experiments of their own is the way to deeper thinking.

Make some mistakes and explain that it's okay. Reflect, take the learning and move on. The only way we can understand what another learner is thinking is to engage them in a rich and purposeful dialogue.

In the words of Matthew Lipman, a leading education theorist, "Reasoning is sharpened and perfected by disciplined discussion as by nothing else."[15]

Note: even when a child doesn't seem like they are listening, remember their filters. They are designed to believe that input from parents and caregivers is important. Even when they're not listening, they are. They can't help it.

First Day at School

A millionbillionwillion miles from home
Waiting for the bell to go. (To go where?)
Why are they all so big, other children?
So noisy? So much at home they
Must have been born in uniform
Spent the years inventing games
That don't let me in. Games
That are rough, that swallow you up
And the railings,
All around, the railings.
Are they to keep out wolves and monsters?
Things that carry off and eat children?
Things you don't take sweets from?
Perhaps they're to stop us getting out
Running away from the lessins.
What does a lessin look like?
Sounds small and slimy.
They keep them in the glassrooms.
Whole rooms made out of glass. Imagine.
I wish I could remember my name
Mummy said it would come in useful.
Like wellies. When there's puddles.
Yellowwellies. I wish she was here.
I think my name is sewn on somewhere
Perhaps the teacher will read it for me.
Tea-cher. The one who makes the tea.

Roger McGough

Better School Success

"Learning is not compulsory. Neither is survival."
W. Edwards Deming

A child who is able to process information in an appropriate way will be able to learn how to use filters in their brain to make better learning decisions.
They will be able to:
- Learn more efficiently
- Process information quicker
- Focus on what's really important in a class
- Perform better in tests
- Engage in productive dialogue
- Have the ability to see multiple "right" answers

Without undue care, schooling can be something that examines the knowledge a child has acquired. What we see more and more is teachers understanding the learning process. Each learner is a unique individual so, as parents, we are faced with a dilemma: Unique Individual vs. Curriculum Needs.

The good news is that learners can learn how to learn and how to educate themselves; this way they will increasingly be able to create a strong future for themselves as a 21st Century Learner.

By learning about the way they learn, they will be able to learn from any teacher in any subject.

Better relationships

Someone who has learned how to learn has more flexibility in the way they think. This enables them to create and establish fruitful long-term relationships. The more they can reflect on the experiences they have with others and the world around them, the more they will be able to create worthwhile outcomes for themselves and others.

When a person is able to think creatively, critically and collaboratively, they are able to:
- Get along with more people
- Stay open to new ideas and people
- Learn from others easily
- Focus on what is important
- Be more "reason-able" when faced with negative information

When we can filter this information in a positive way, we won't make relationship decisions based on the past. You could look at a relationship as something occurring right now.

From that viewpoint, more unbiased decisions are possible and the ups and the downs of relationships might become avoidable.

Relationships with the world around us can have a more effective future, when viewed through the filter of the 3Cs mentioned above (Critical, Creative, and Collaborative). Working smarter now leads to less work later.

Learning new tricks

Following is the earliest reference we can find for the saying "you can't teach an old dog new tricks":

> "...and he [a shepherd] muste teche his dogge to barke whan he wolde haue hym, to ronne whan he wold haue hym, and to leue ronning whan he wolde haue hym; or els he is not a cunninge shepeherd. The dogge must lerne it, whan he is a whelpe, or els it will not be: for it is harde to make an olde dogge to stoupe."[16]

Here you realise very quickly that the author is actually talking about his dog, when in reality he is showing is his beliefs about how he thinks. Current brain research would disagree with this "finding". Plasticity, or neuroplasticity, is the lifelong ability of the brain to reorganise neural pathways based on new experiences. As we learn, we acquire new knowledge and skills through instruction or experience. In order to learn or memorise a fact or skill, there must be persistent functional changes in the brain that represent the new knowledge. This is the ability of the brain to change with learning.

When you form a thought and you hold onto that thought for a long period of time, you need to work harder in order to change that habit or thought process.

Think about a habit you have right now. Say that you smoke and that you've done so for twenty years. At a pack a day, that means you have been lifting a cigarette to your mouth twenty times a day over the course of 7,300 days. This is a habit that is ingrained in your brain.

Your body accepts this as a behaviour that you do every day and it will be hard to change the more years you have under your belt. It is not impossible, but it is harder.

If you were to change a child's thinking patterns today, the opposite will occur. Instead of having to try to teach positive patterns, it will be more difficult to introduce negative patterns, no matter how many outside influences may be available.

You want to make sure your kid's mind is set for life, not just ready for the next test.

Can default settings be overcome?

The short answer is yes! No matter how young or old your children are, it might be difficult to see whether it's possible to stop the way they think or to change the way they think.

Time and time again, science and case studies have pointed out that kids are able to learn a new learning process. They are able to learn how to take in new pieces of information and process them in new ways. They are able to create a completely different thinking pattern by being exposed to lots of different experiences.

Other reasons behind the "yes" include:

The brain is malleable

Some studies are showing that the brain is able to change, even when it seems that the way a person thinks has been handed down over generations. The brain is not a static organ. Just like other organs in the body, it too changes with the passage of time. As the scientist Marvin Minsky suggests, "The principal activities of brains are making changes in themselves."[17]

Practice makes perfect

It's been shown that a person who practices a new habit again and again is able to change the way that they act.[18] If you change the way you do something, then you will begin to learn in a new way. And the more it happens, the more you will revert to the new behaviour over the old one. Ensure that the practice is effective otherwise you may be repeating poor practice over and over.

When motivation is high, success is higher

If a child or their parent is motivated to create change, it can be seen that the results are more long term. For example, if a learner wants to be a better student; they will automatically work harder in order to change the way they study, for example.

David McClelland is a pioneer in work-place motivation and according to him there are three basic motivational traits that people display:

1. **Power**—People do things because they are "authority motivated". This driver produces a need to be influential, effective and to make an impact. There is a strong need to lead and for their ideas to prevail. There is also motivation and need towards increasing personal status and prestige.
2. **Achievement**—People who are "achievement motivated" seek achievement, attainment of realistic but challenging goals, and advancement. There is a strong need for feedback as to achievement and progress, and a need for a sense of accomplishment.
3. **Affiliation**—People who are "affiliation motivated", have a need for friendly relationships and are motivated towards interaction with other people. The affiliation driver produces motivation, a need to be liked and held in popular regard. These people are team players.

Do you know what your drivers are?

What are the drivers for other members of your family, and for your kids?

Does this explain some of their behaviour? Because if you understand the motivation behind the behaviour, then you can better influence the results.

Emotional Competence

Emotional intelligence was originally developed by the psychologists Peter Salovey, John Mayer and Howard Gardner and became popular when Daniel Goleman wrote a book titled <u>Emotional Intelligence</u>.[19]

In simple terms emotional intelligence is our ability to control our emotions and understand and express feelings in a way that is positive to both ourselves and those around us.

In the past, people were assessed by conventional intellect, which was referred to as IQ. What emotional intelligence tells us is that there are broader aspects to intelligence and we need EQ or Emotional Quotient as well as IQ to succeed.

To be successful we must be able not only to understand ourselves, our goals, intentions, responses and behaviour, but also to understand others, and their feelings.
There are five domains of emotional intelligence:

Intrapersonal:
- Self-awareness
- Self-management
- Self-motivation

Interpersonal:
- Empathy
- Managing Relationships

What is self-efficacy?

According to Albert Bandura, a former professor of Science in
Psychology at Stanford University, self-efficacy is "the belief in
one's capabilities to organize and execute the courses of
action required to manage prospective situations."[20] What
does that mean? Self-efficacy is your belief in your ability to
succeed. Bandura described these principles as factors of
how people think, behave and feel.

As Bandura and other researchers have shown, self-efficacy
affects everything from psychological states and behaviour to
attitudes and motivation.

Most people can identify things they want to achieve in their
lives and things they would like to change. But, many of us
find difficulty in completing these plans. Bandura and others
have found that an individual's self-efficacy plays a major role
in how goals, tasks, and challenges are approached. Matt
Hudson, the co-author of this book, has dedicated an entire
book (The Saboteur Within) to the intricacies of the
unconscious mind and how it plays a significant role within any
change process.[21]

Bandura suggests that children with a strong sense of self-
efficacy:
  • See challenging tasks as difficulties to be overcome
  • Cultivate a deeper interest in the things they study
  • Are committed to their interests and activities
  • Show more resilience when faced with disappointments
    and obstructions

People with lesser developed self-efficacy:
  • Eschew challenging tasks
  • Believe they are incapable of approaching difficult tasks
    and situations
  • Are pre-occupied with their own thoughts about failing
  • Show little resilience and lose confidence quickly

So how does self-efficacy develop, and more importantly, how can we help instill it in our children?

It begins to develop in early childhood as kids cope with a wide range of experiences. This growth continues to progress throughout life as they acquire new attitudes, skills and knowledge. With this in mind, how do you show them resilience? When the lid doesn't come off a jar of pickles do you persist or give up? When life gives you lemons do you make lemonade?

Four specific sources of self-efficacy

1. Mastery Experiences
Bandura explains that "performing a task successfully strengthens our sense of self-efficacy. However, failing to adequately deal with a task or challenge can undermine and weaken self-efficacy."

2. Social Modeling
"Seeing people similar to oneself succeed by sustained effort raises observers' beliefs that they too possess the capabilities master comparable activities to succeed."

3. Social Persuasion
Bandura also suggests that people could be persuaded to believe that they have the skills and capabilities to succeed.

4. Psychological Responses
Moods, emotional states, physical reactions, and stress levels are all context specific and can adversely affect performance in a particular situation.

As with the child and the dog experience the meaning that the child makes is personal and unique to the child, built upon their own personal experience and beliefs about the event. The emotional state that is connected to the event will also have an impact on a child's performance in other areas of their life that may be in some way connected to the original stimulus.

Learning is therefore enhanced by a challenge but weakened by a threat.

Threats release cortisol into the system, limiting our ability to engage in higher order thinking. Tasks that require active processing by your child, will improve recall, and if that is experienced as enjoyable it will create deeper learning.

The Truth about Change

"Change is the only constant" – Heraclitus

Have you ever experienced the unexpected? Change can create huge stresses on a person as the brain has a primitive part, which is similar to most animals, called the limbic system. This basic setup is described by Evian Gordon, a neuroscientist, as "the fundamental organising principle of the brain," which seeks to "minimise danger and maximise reward". Your neurological system is instantly fired up, to figure out if the change is a danger to you or if it will reward you. Therefore the more meanings your child can draw from experiences the more resilient they will be when changes occur.

Changes afford you and your children:
- The chance to grow—When your kids aren't limited to one way of thinking, they have the tools to argue effectively and to challenge the thinking behind ideas and not the person offering the ideas.
- The chance to have new concepts—A person who is able to learn in a creative way will feel open to have new ideas and new trains of thought.
- The chance to adapt—Since learning is something that

often happens in new situations, the 21st Century Learner will be able to adapt to any number of new situations and possibilities.[22]

- The chance to challenge—Learning isn't just about rote memorisation, but also the challenging of ideas so that the child can understand more clearly the purpose of the learning they are currently engaged in.

Dr. Gordon also established Brain Revolution, a not-for-profit organisation empowering underprivileged children around the world with insights and fun games to discover and train their brains. For more information, go to www.brainrevolution.org.

Creating Learning Climates

"Learning is everywhere and it's messy!"
John Medina

When your children take charge, you are creating opportunities for them to create their own positive settings. As you begin to teach your offspring new ways of experiencing the world, you can encourage them to begin to understand the world in a new way.

They will not be limited to just what they know or what their friends tell them to know. In your role as a parent you have more influence than you realise. By adopting this mindset you encourage your children to:

Feel safe

A child who doesn't have any boundaries is one who might not know whether they are safe and protected by you. When you establish boundaries and you help by making them aware, they will not feel like they are being set adrift in the ocean by themselves.

Take chances

When you support the learning process, you will begin to see them take chances. Though they know the boundaries and guidelines, they will also feel like they can try things out, make some mistakes, see how they work, and then assess their progress.

Learn from past experiences

Since they might not have a lot of past experiences from which to draw, you will want to provide your kids with as many as possible. Though they might learn in a different way, as they get older, the more you can encourage them to have rich and valuable experiences, the more they will learn.

No matter how you decide to influence your children, or not, you are always influential. Even if they simply ignore you, they have made a conscious decision to ignore you.
Remember: You cannot not communicate

"Don't worry that children never listen to you;
worry that they are always watching you."
Robert Fulghum

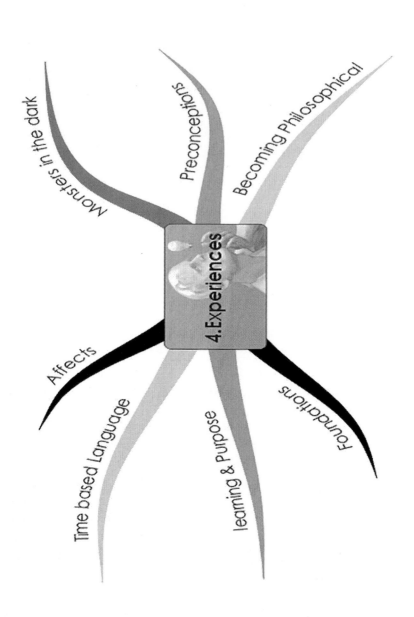

Monsters in the dark

Preconceptions

Becoming Philosophical

4.Experiences

Affects

Time based Language

learning & Purpose

Foundations

Chapter 4
Experiences

"I believe in everything until it's disproved. So I believe in fairies, myths, dragons. It all exists, even if it's in your mind. Who's to say that dreams and nightmares aren't as real as the here and now?"
John Lennon

Monsters in the Dark

Wendy telephoned me and explained how Lucy, her eleven-year-old daughter, had been having night terrors since she was five years of age and the doctors were now offering to prescribe drugs to help. This caused Mum to seek me out, via a personal referral from a GP whose child I had worked with previously.

If this had been a less complex issue and Lucy had been younger, then I would have pointed her in the direction of Carl-Johan Forssén Ehrlin and his new audio book, which is an excellent way to get children to sleep; I am yawning right now as I think about it.[23]

But, Lucy's problem was now impacting on the whole family as she would read a book until she was really tired and then fall asleep naturally, but after sleeping for about an hour or so she would wake up and scream the house down. Mum and Dad would take her into their bed and calm her down until she would eventually doze off again.

So, Mum, Dad, Lucy's younger sister and Lucy herself were getting no proper rest.

Lucy sat at the side of me and I asked her when she knew it was time to scare herself? Her eyes flicked up for a second, then she bowed her head and replied, "I don't know". In that small instance, I had one of my Sherlock Holmes moments and, as a result, I now had enough information to help my client in what would probably only take a few minutes.

"Did you move house, when you were about four or five years old?" I asked. "Yes," replied Lucy and Wendy at the same time.

"And was your first bedroom very bright and light or perhaps you moved around September?" Lucy stared at her mother for input, as she wasn't too sure.

"Yes and Yes, but what has that got to do with this?" asked a very inquisitive mother.

"Basically," I explained, "Lucy has the image of her current bedroom as being dark and scary. She reads at night to keep her eyes from flicking up and accessing that terrifying image inside her mind..." Then, directing my voice to Lucy, I said: "The same image that you just looked at when you sat down". Mum sat, open-mouthed, whilst Lucy nodded her head.

There are many ways to shift an image or to change the meaning or a person's perceptions (see the section on NLP). I chose an improvised swish pattern* putting my hand up and in front of Lucy at the same spot that she held this dark and scary, imaginary image. Palm flat, I had Lucy stare at the image and then I turned my hand a quarter turn, so that Lucy could only see the tops of my fingertips. In effect turning the image sideways on so that she was unable to see it.

"Now, try to feel bad and try in vain to see the image," I chuckled, as did a very happy Lucy.

A few weeks later Wendy called to say thank you and to tell me that Lucy was still okay and sleeping well in her own bed.

"But why didn't anyone else pick this up sooner?" she asked

"Perhaps, because no one else was looking for the simple solution, which was staring them in the face," I replied with a dash of fun.

My Sherlock Holmes moment explained: When I asked Lucy about her problem, her eyes flashed upwards and she went from looking at me to staring down at her lap. This told me there was something in her mind's eye that was frightening her. This was only happening at bedtime.

Scary images are normally dark and large and if Lucy is in her bedroom and managing to scare herself, she must be shrinking, in the dark, inside her mind. I deduced therefore that in order for her to be smaller she must have been younger when this imprint first began.

An imprint is created with a change of circumstance as the human brain scans for sameness for security and safety. Therefore there must have been a change in her environment, which triggered an amygdala response resulting in the imprint. Many years after the imprint first formed, Lucy was still having the same problem because it hadn't been re-written. Until now. Elementary, my dear Watson![24]

Preconceptions

There are two different arguments that are brought up when it comes to learning and development: nurture and nature.

Our understanding of the brain and learning has undergone the type of evolutionary change described by the American philosopher and scientist Thomas Kuhn in his seminal work The Structure of Scientific Revolutions.[25] Like other major changes, this has been a radical one. Moving us from guessing, observing and conjecture, to research and imaging; we can actually see the inner workings of the brain.

Tick...tock...

Historically, our understanding of mind and body, nature and nurture, has existed as a dilemma, either implicitly, as in Plato, more mechanically, as in Aristotle, or, most notably, in the philosophy of Descartes. As Dr. Michael Stone, a professor of clinical psychiatry at Columbia observed in Healing the Mind, we have moved from speculation to biological psychiatry.[26] Albert Einstein told the story about a watch:

"In our endeavour to understand reality we are somewhat like a man trying to understand the mechanism of a closed watch. He sees the face and the moving hands, even hears its ticking, but has no way of opening the case. If he is a genius he may form some picture of a mechanism which could be responsible for all of the things he observes, but he may never be quite sure his picture is the only one which could explain his observations."[27]

To use Einstein's metaphor we are now able to open the watch and explore the wonders of the internal mechanism. The same can be said of parents understanding their children, we can only hope that what we are imparting to them has the desired effect, but our observations are uniquely personal to us and we can only be the observer of our own observations.

Plato and Descartes proposed that certain things are inborn, or that they just happen naturally regardless of external influences. John Locke, the 17th Century philosopher, believed in what is known as 'tabula rasa', (literally the 'blank slate'). This would mean all that we are, including our knowledge, is determined by our own experiences.

So, when a person attains academic success, did they do so because of their genes or is it because of a rich learning environment? Today, the majority of experts believe that behaviour and development are influenced by both nature and nurture. But there are still some un-answered questions within the area of what influences intelligence.

Becoming More Philosophical

There are many rich concepts in the world, for children to explore. For example:
- Ethics
- Good and evil
- Logic
- Math
- Cause and effect
- Greater beings
- Danger

Encourage your kids to ask questions about rich concepts, talk together about the questions and what was interesting or puzzling for them in the questions?

What kind of questions are they, collect them and display them when you can.

Play "spot the assumptions" in the questions with them.
Get philosophical—it's fun!

We are all learners and we are always learning. Following some of the advice in this book can help you to become a more effective learner again. Keeping this in mind will make all of the steps you take to encourage them to learn all the easier.

You aren't going to be fighting to teach them what they need to know. You will be building upon their own innate knowledge as well as their own desire to find out what the world has to offer.

"The aim of a thinking skills programmes like P4C is not to turn children into philosophers but to help them become more thoughtful, more reflective more considerate, and more reasonable individuals".[28]
Matthew Lipman

Foundations for Cognitive Learning

Brain research tells us that when the fun stops, learning often stops too.

"Most children can't wait to start nursery and approach the beginning of school with awe and anticipation. KS1 learners often talk passionately about what they learn and do in school. Unfortunately, the current emphasis on standardised testing and rote learning encroaches upon many students' joy.

In their zeal to raise test scores, too many policymakers wrongly assume that students who are laughing, interacting in groups, or being creative with art, music, or dance are not doing real academic work. The result is that some professionals feel pressure to preside over more sedate classrooms with students on the same page in the same book, sitting in straight rows, facing straight ahead." Attributed to Judy Willis.[29]

A child is capable of learning any number of things as they grow.

While they are going to have some innate knowledge, when they need to learn something new, they will go about trying to learn more.

Put a piece of unusual food in front of your child to see how they learn:
- They will look at it first.
- Then they will smell it.
- They might touch it.
- Then they might bring it up to their face.
- Then they will taste it.
- If they like it, they will eat it. If they don't like it, they will spit it out.

This is a simple process of testing what's in front of them and then finding out what to do next.

Learning, is something that allows your child to take these lessons to heart:
- What they should eat
- What they should do to get attention
- What they need to do in order to move around
- What they do in order to walk
- What they might say in order to receive something specific
- How to eat
- How to crawl

This list could be an entire book long. Children are learning how to interpret the world and the things that occur around them. While they might not know what the importance is of everything around them, the more they explore their world, the more they will be able to find out.

A child learns to run, to laugh, to talk, to play, to read, to write and so on. When you think about it, they have so much to learn from the time they are young that it's nearly impossible to think of them as being able to do anything but learn.
It's amazing they have time to eat and to grow while learning. But they do.

Observations

When a young child is unable to move around, as they are when they are babies, they will only experience the world in front of them. They are not going to think too much about anything outside of their scope of vision.

But in this vision, they can see people in front of them and they can begin to:
- See how their actions affect others
- See how their body works
- See how their environment changes
- Notice how they interact with their food or with other things in their environment

Just noticing the world around them and seeing what is placed before them is going to help them to begin to see what they are in relation to the world.

At first, we are uncertain whether they really understand they are a part of something bigger or that they have so much more to see behind them and below them.

But the more observing they do, the more they expand their perception.

Mimicking

Children are professionals at mimicking things around them. While some of this mimicking is a part of the learning process, some of it is simply the child trying to see what happens when they do the same thing as someone else. For example, when a child waves they might get a big response. They can feel that others are happy with what they did, so they repeat it. Or they use their innate cause and effect knowledge to continue to do what they see since they know what effect it will have. Mimicking might seem to be thoughtless, but it truly does create a lesson in their mind. When they see their parents do something again and again, for example, they are going to try to make sure they can do this same action too. Even if they're not entirely sure why they are doing it.

Play Time

During playtime, children begin to pick up even more ideas and lessons from the world around them. Using their innate knowledge, they can begin to see that some actions lead to other actions. Or they might begin to use logic to decide what might happen next.

They might also begin to see that certain people act in certain ways, so they will respond accordingly. Or they might simply enjoy the colours and the sounds that come along with playing. In any case, those who are engaged in playtime activities will be able to learn more, even if they seem to just be having fun.

Learning can be fun, you know.
The brain continues to develop when it learns lessons that are associated with positive memories. The more positive the memory (in the way a game can be positive), the easier it is to retain the knowledge and to retrieve it at a later time.

Think back to the games you used to play when you were younger. You probably remember more of them than you thought you did.

"Play also creates the zone of proximal development of the child. In play, the child is always behaving beyond his age, above his usual everyday behaviour; in play he is, as it were, a head above himself," said the Belarusian psychologist, Lev Vygotsky.

"Play contains in a concentrated form, as in the focus of a magnifying glass, all developmental tendencies; it is as if the child tries to jump above his usual level. The relationship of play to development should be compared to the relationship between instruction and development."[30]

Siblings

The siblings and parents of a child will also help to stimulate the learning process. Since siblings have different viewpoints on the world, as they have been around longer than a younger brother or sister, they can help to add more influence to the kid's life.

They might give them an opportunity to interact with something the child might not have chosen to interact with on their own.

In fact, the more people that can be around a child, the better. They will be exposed to more ideas and more actions. Instead of just learning how they react, they will see others interact. This can teach them about social rules and relationships, for example.

As kids progress through life, they might change their ideas about relationships, but their family and others around them are the first part of the learning process.
Children have a lot to learn from the start of their lives, but they do have a lot of help.

When a family is dedicated to helping a child learn, and they understand the best times for a child to learn, that is very valuable to the child.

A Safe Place to Learn

The home can provide a safe place where learning, thinking, emotional comfort, and pleasure as well as knowledge are experienced. When the family uses strategies to reduce stress and build a positive emotional environment, children gain emotional resilience and learn more efficiently and at higher levels of cognition. Brain-imaging studies support this relationship.

After all, a child who learns quickly can be a valuable part of the family dynamic and they can begin to create their own sense of self-identity. That is the goal of growing up.

When a Child Learns (Purpose?)

According to John Medina, the developmental molecular biologist we spoke about earlier on in the Brain Rules section, explains that many well-meaning parents, caregivers and teachers think their child's brain is interested in learning. "That is not accurate," according to him. "The brain is not interested in learning. The brain is interested in surviving. Every ability in our intellectual tool kit was engineered to escape extinction.

Learning exists only to serve the requirements of this primal goal. It is a happy coincidence that our intellectual tools can do double duty in the classroom, conferring on us the ability to create spreadsheets and speak French. But that's not the brain's day job.

That is an incidental by-product of a much deeper force: the gnawing, clawing desire to live to the next day. We do not survive so that we can learn. We learn so that we can survive."[31]

Myth busting

As parents we need reliable facts, not myths based on hearsay and rumour. What to believe? Dependable science can help us:

Myth 1: Playing Mozart to an unborn child increases their mathematical ability.

> **Fact:** Once born, children will simply remember Mozart along with other sights sounds and smells from the womb. You would do better to encourage impulse control and their ability to delay gratification.

Myth 2: Language DVDs boost your kids' vocabulary.

> **Fact:** Such DVDs can actually reduce it, but the words that you use will boost both vocabulary and IQ.

Myth 3: Learning French before the age of 3 plus a room full of brain friendly toys and educational DVDs will boost brain development.

> **Fact:** A cardboard box, some crayons and your time will be far more beneficial. The worst thing is the flat screen TV in your lounge!

Myth 4: Telling kids they are "smart" will boost their confidence.

> **Fact:** Such praise can actually make them less willing to rise to challenge. Focus on their effort and determination instead.

Myth 5: Young children are "naturally" happy.

Fact: New friendships and the ability to develop an understanding of nonverbal communication is much more beneficial. Texting may destroy this ability. Learning a musical instrument will develop it.

Specific Learning

The Swiss developmental psychologist Jean Piaget observed that between the ages of two and four, children were unable to manipulate and transform information in logical ways and were able to think in image and symbol.[32]

"I don't like it," the 3-year-old muttered to herself as the guests left. Miserable throughout her older sister's birthday party, she was now growing angry. "I want Ally's doll, not this one!" Her parents had bought her a consolation present, but the strategy went down like a bomb. The girl threw her doll to the floor. "Ally's doll! Ally's doll!" She began to cry. You can imagine a parent making any of several choices in the face of this bubbling brew.

"You seem sad. Are you sad?" is what the girl's dad said. The little girl nodded, still angry, too. The dad continued. "I think I know why. You're sad because Ally's got all the presents. You only got one!" The little girl nodded again. "You want the same number and you can't have it, and that's unfair and that makes you sad." The dad seemed to be pouring it on.
"Whenever somebody gets something I want and I don't, I get sad, too."There was Silence. Then the dad said the line most characteristic of a verbalising parent.

"We have a word for that feeling, honey," he said. "Do you want to know what that word is?"
She whimpered, "OK." He held her in his arms.
"We call it being jealous. You wanted Ally's presents, and you couldn't have them. You were jealous."

She cried softly but was beginning to calm down.

"Jealous," she whispered.

"Yep," Dad replied, "and it's an icky feeling."

"I been jealous all day," she replied, nestling into her daddy's big strong arms.

This big-hearted father is firstly good at labelling his feelings and secondly at teaching his daughter to label hers. He knows what sadness in his own heart feels like and announces it easily. He knows what sadness in his child's heart looks like, and he is teaching her to announce it, too. He is also good at teaching joy, anger, disgust, concern, fear—the entire spectrum of his little girl's experience.

Research shows that this labelling habit is a dominant behaviour for all parents who raise happy children. Kids who are exposed to this parenting behaviour on a regular basis become better at self-soothing, are more able to focus on tasks, and have more successful peer relationships. Sometimes knowing what to do is tougher than knowing what to say. But sometimes saying is all that's needed.

Notice in the story that as the dad addressed his daughter's feelings directly, the little girl began to calm down. This is a common finding; you can measure it in the laboratory. Verbalising has a soothing effect on the nervous system of children. (Adults, too.) Thus, this Brain Rule: Labelling emotions calms big feelings.

Milton Erickson, the internationally acclaimed leading practitioner of medical hypnosis, utilised a similar linguistic approach as above, in the form of "truisms" which are "an objectively verifiable fact, or something that the patient already believed to be true."[33] By acknowledging the child's reality we allow them to feel heard, accepted and understood, which leads them naturally to being able to trust us.

Here's what we think is going on in the brain. Verbal and nonverbal communication is like two interlocking neurological systems. Infants' brains haven't yet connected these systems very well. Their bodies can feel fear, disgust and joy way before their brains can talk about them. This means that children will experience the physiological characteristics of emotional responses before they know what those responses are.

That's why large feelings are often scary for little people (tantrums often self-feed because of this fear). That's not a sustainable gap. Kids will need to find out what's going on with their big feelings, however scary they seem at first. They need to connect these two neurological systems.

Researchers believe that learning to label emotions provides the linkage. The earlier this bridge gets constructed, the more likely you are to see self-soothing behaviours, along with a large raft of other benefits. Researcher Carroll Izard has shown that in households that do not provide such instruction, these nonverbal and verbal systems remain somewhat disconnected or integrate in unhealthy ways.[34] Without labels to describe the feelings they have, a child's emotional life can remain a confusing cacophony of physiological experiences.

Jean Piaget, who observed that kids between two and four think in images and symbols, also noticed that between the ages of four and seven kids tend to become very curious and ask many questions; they begin the use of primitive reasoning. The 'Why, why, why?' questions begin. There is an emergence in the interest of reasoning and wanting to know why things are the way they are. When your child begins constantly asking, "Why? Why? Why?" they are busy creating meanings and connections, so take your time to ensure you help them to make the best understandings possible.

Sometimes the meaning a child makes may result in unusual behaviour, a bad habit or even physiological problems. Time based language can be very useful to overcome these issues.

Time Based Language

Time-based language is when you presuppose that by the time your child is X years old he or she will be able to do Y, because that's how it was for Mum or Dad and or Grandma and Granddad. This strategy has been used successfully by Matt, with many young clients over the years to overcome, behavioural issues, bed-wetting, stammering, eczema, asthma, poor spelling and countless number of childhood allergies and phobias. You see, a child's mind is wide open to you as a parent, teacher or guardian, and by practicing time-based language, you too will be able to help your child progress, more comfortably beyond these minor hang-ups.

Time-based language example

Mary is four years old and still in nappies, so mum and dad might say: "I was the same as you Mary, until I was four and a half (marking out a point in the near future for the change to take place). And one day I woke up with a dry bed (highlighting the dry bed, which is the intended outcome).

Caleb is 12 years old and is suffering with low self-esteem owing to being overweight, the conversation went like this: "That is a problem that you have had up until now and I too had had the same problem, yet when my 13th birthday came (future date again), the fat seemed to just vanish and I began to enjoy exercise and making better lifestyle choices."

Rapport is always a main quality of the dialogue and key to any behavioural intervention. Children need to be encouraged to extend their knowledge further than their experience.

As they are beginning to use their knowledge from specific thoughts, they will start to ask questions. A lot of questions. During this phase, a child will begin to gather knowledge from the answers they get to these questions. And while you might begin to tire of the questions, this is the way that children connect their knowledge to some sort of answer to a problem.

They will begin to create a system of rules in their brain that can then be used as they play or interact with others.

What affects me?

During this stage the brain only cares about survival issues that may pose a threat:
- Will this affect me?
- Do I like this?
- What do I think about this?
- Do I need to run away?
- Should I fight?
- Should I cry?

Simple questions for a child to consider, and they don't need or want to know anything more outside of these concerns. Joanne is five years old and in a playground conflict, she tries out a range of emotional responses.

She shouts and it fails. She hits and is hit back harder. Failing again she cries and everything stops, the teacher comes to her rescue. Success!

Tears work. Joanne is now 43 years old and embroiled in an office confrontation.

She "cries" and everything stops, her manager comes to her rescue. Success!

But is it a success when you are an adult yet still using your childhood response patterns? Ah, but remember: The brain isn't bothered about appropriate behaviour, it's focused on survival.

Data entry

According to Jean Piaget, in what he termed the "Concrete Operational Phase", children can think logically about objects and events between the ages of seven to eleven. However other psychologists like Vygotsky, Gardner and our own personal experience suggests that this can happen considerably earlier.

Younger children are more than capable of speculating about meaning. Engaging them in meaningful dialogues about rich concepts is beneficial to the brain and their understanding of the world.

A rich concept should encourage your child to use all of their thinking tools and strategies through provocative topics, they might include identity, values, choice and truth, and lead your child into thoughtful guided discussion.

As a result, children are able to make choices that use their knowledge and their experience. By challenging their thinking and their use of language with what might be termed Socratic questioning, we are encouraging attributes that is outlined by Matthew Lipman, who is generally credited as the founder of Philosophy for Children, or P4C, through his decision to bring philosophy to young people.[35]

Children are able to begin to create multiple answers to questions. "The aim of a thinking skills programme such as P4C is not to turn children into philosophers, but to help them become more thoughtful, more reflective, more considerate and more reason-able individuals," Lipman explains.

The root of the word education is *educare*. It comes from Latin, and combines the two words, *ex* and *ducere*. These translate as, to draw out of, lead out of, and similar. The Romans believed educating to be synonymous with drawing knowledge out of somebody or leading them out of regular thinking. Or, as Winston Churchill put it:

"My education was interrupted only by my schooling."

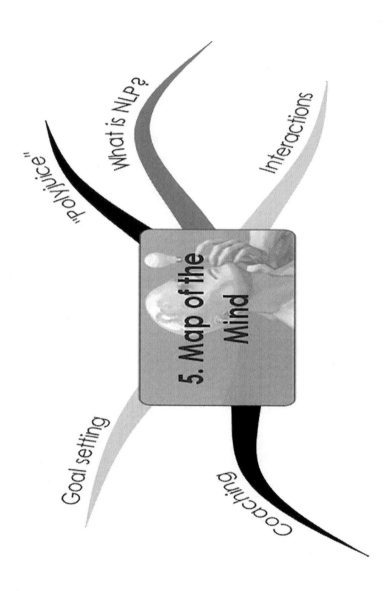

"PolYjuice"

What is NLP?

Interactions

5. Map of the Mind

Goal setting

Coaching

Chapter 5
The Map of the Mind

*"To be in your children's memories tomorrow,
You have to be in their lives today."*
Barbara Johnson

Hogwarts and the Polyjuice Spell

I was invited into a school to work with a young girl who was thought to have Asperger's. As the Deputy Head (DH) and I walked to the office, where the girl was (let's call her Mary), the DH remarked: "We can't get anything out of this girl, she just seems to live in a Harry Potter world all of her own, isolating herself from everyone else".

I nodded knowingly, without knowing anything at all. We entered the room and DH said, "Mary, Mister Hudson. Mister Hudson, Mary." Then she turned on her heels and leaving the door ajar, went into the room next door.

Mary was sitting with her head down and hadn't even acknowledged that I was in the room. Remembering the information that I had been given about her, I turned and closed the door, keeping my back to Mary. As I did so, I exclaimed, in my best Brian Blessed voice, "You have never met the likes of me before child...! For I do magic!" Mary excitedly broke her silence.

"Like Harry Potter?" I quickly spun round, stared into her eyes, brought my right hand up to my face and, whilst tapping my nose a couple of times, I spoke more gently, "But not outside of Hogwarts, eh?"

I quickly sat next to Mary and explained that I needed her to imagine Harry Potter taking a vial of Polyjuice and appearing to the whole world as Mary.

Harry would attend classes, make all kinds of new friends, have many fun conversations and all the while Mary and I, both hidden under a cloak of invisibility, would follow close behind him, observing how he was able to be so friendly, so open and so likeable. "No one else can know about this, especially Muggles (non-magic folk)!" Mary smiled and agreed.

I then stood up and pointed to the door, again in my Brian Blessed voice, I boomed: "Now go child and open the door to a whole new world."

Mary left the room with a spring in her step. That would be my first and last encounter with Mary as the DH continued to mention to me, weeks, months and even years later: "I can't believe the transformation in that girl, she became outgoing and simply transformed."

When reading this story it may appear overly simple to influence a child. And it is, but that doesn't mean it is easy. Yet, as you learn the skills in this book and better understand the mind it will soon become a part of your regular "tool kit". Please remember Matt has many years tucked under his behavioural change belt. For more examples of his work, please see The Saboteur Within, Matt's book on self-sabotage and the power of the subconscious mind.

In the beginning, you learned how the brain worked and how it processes information. With NLP, you can begin to see how this process can be adjusted.

What is NLP?

Neuro-Linguistic Programming, NLP, is the practice of "programming" the mind to act and react in a different way.

Developed in the 1970s, by Gestalt therapist Richard Bandler and linguist John Grinder, NLP was originally a modeling exercise designed to discover the structure of excellence.[36] This learning would go on to help people achieve success in all areas of life, including relationships, families, education, sports, work, sales and more.

When NLP tools and techniques are used, people of all ages can begin to see their life change.

What's interesting about NLP is that it works with the idea of modeling. When you model the success of someone else, you will create a basis for better behaviour and better results.

For example, when you practice the idea of focusing on what a child is doing well, you will encourage that behaviour. When you create the model of interacting with others in a positive way that promotes safety and respect, you will encourage others around you to do the same.

By using a certain model of behaviour, you will begin to create a new reality for yourself and for those around you. This doesn't mean all of your problems will go away, but you will be able to approach them in a new and effective way.

As a result you will communicate better, learn more effectively, interact with others positively, create personal change and forge stronger bonds.

This is not a set of practices that work as gimmicks either. NLP uses the way the brain works and processes information in order to create a new response. When you create a new response, you can create a snowball effect of responses and of results that allow you to continue to see positive life events.

Children benefit the most from these practices as they are incorporating these ideas into their still-developing mind. Kids are able to integrate these NLP practices not just as new habits, but as the way they interact in the world. No matter what they might experience, they will be able to enjoy the results, knowing they are working with their mind, not against it.

How does NLP work?

NLP works in a very specific way. By recognising the value of the way our nervous systems work, NLP allows a person to change the way the body handles all of the experiences we have. And each moment is an experience, after all.

Let's break down the words that make up NLP in order to make things a little clearer.

N = Neuro

Neuro is the term that refers to the brain's processes. When we learn a new idea, we create a new connection in the brain. When we return to this idea again and again, we begin to create a pattern, which then creates a habit and a subsequent action and reaction to certain conditions. In other words, what we do a lot, we will come back to.

The way our body and brain responds to certain situations is stored in the brain. And all of our brains work differently because our experiences are different.

When we realise this, we can begin to understand that it's not about changing the experiences we have, but it's about changing our responses to the experiences we have. We have the choice to change.

Your children have the choice to change, once they realise they are the ones who change themselves. This is not a process in which you will give your child a number of tools and everything will be okay.

They will need to use the tools, see how they work, and then their brain will make the changes it needs to make in order to see the results they want to see.

Others have said that it's not about "how" a person changes, but it's "what" the person changes.

For example, if a person stops smoking by taking a form of medication, does that make it any less positive than if they quit smoking cold turkey? Not at all. The results are the same, but one person's brain responded to the quitting process in one way, while another responded in another way.
Results are what matter.

L = Linguistic

The words we use every day change the way we experience the world. If you've ever had a bad day, think back on it. Maybe you got out of bed and stubbed your toe on a toy and thought to yourself, "Oh, this is going to be a bad day".

If you had laughed about the incident instead, you might not have given it any second thought. But if you continued to remind yourself of how bad a day you were having, some other things might have drifted into your awareness, and you noticed that a lot of things didn't go the way you wanted them to.

These negative events confirm your initial thought that you were going to have a bad day and then, shockingly, you did have a bad day.

The words you choose to define your experiences will change the way you experience the world. No matter what might actually be happening, we interpret the world based on the way we have experienced it before.

So, if you always have a bad day when you go to a certain place, you think in terms of the association of this past experience. This causes you to have a bad day, regardless of what might actually be happening on that particular day.

If your child always associates school as a time of frustration, then they are going to associate the idea of frustration with learning. Though this might not seem like a realistic connection, it's a connection they will make anyway. Because it's their experience.

One could say we define the world in words, but NLP helps you develop a new vocabulary that produces more effective and positive results.

P = Programming

Finally, and this is not surprising to most, programming is the final key to the idea of NLP.

When you can program the brain to focus on new ways that symbols in the world interact with us, you can begin to see new results and you can have new experiences.

Think of a child who is programmed to think everything is positive and everything is abundant in their lives. They don't even consider the idea of negativity and they don't consider the idea of disparity. Imagine what a child such as that could achieve.

"Programming" has often been linked to ideas like brainwashing and other similarly negative concepts, and as a result some people have a hard time relating to this process. The way we use the word "programming" in NLP, is nothing more than introducing new ways of interpreting the world. And the introduction of new ideas is not a bad thing, it's just a process.

By looking at experiences in a new way, you can react in a new way, which leads to different results, and so on. Through the use of NLP your child will begin to see the world through a new set of eyes, a set of eyes that is able to look at challenges not as bad things, but as opportunities for growth. These tools are not just to be applied at school, they can create a whole new way of living for your child.

NLP terms to know and understand

Whether you are completely new to NLP or not, it is important that you understand and to review the basic terms that will be used as you continue to read this book.

Some of these terms are simple, while others may not be as familiar. The more of these concepts you understand, the even more effective the NLP techniques will be.

Anchor

This is a state the mind returns to when it needs to learn something or remember something. Help your child find an anchor they can return to so they can have a positive experience.

For example, when your child is fearful during a test, you might teach them to go to a memory that is positive for them, like when they first learned how to play a new videogame that tested their skills, and which they now consistently get the top score in.

They will anchor into this state and bring up positive emotions and feelings. These feelings will then eventually be linked with test taking and they will lose their overall fear.

Congruence

A child may not need to know this term, but it's the overall goal of NLP. By bringing the different parts of the brain into congruence, a child can be the most effective person they can be. When their actions, their values and their reactions are congruent, they will be more powerful in their lives.

Framing

When you walk into any situation, you have certain assumptions about it. As you first read the title of this book, you created a set of assumptions. Were you to be told that this was the most amazing book ever, you would have been even more excited to read it. But if you were told that this was a really boring book, that frame would have coloured your entire experience. How you frame things for your child and how your child frames their experience impacts how they interact in the world.

Parts

These are exactly what they sound like—parts of the way a person acts and interacts. Your child might have a part that is playful at home, unruly at school, and so on. Depending on where they are, they might have a different part that comes out. The goal of NLP is to ensure that all of the parts are the same, no matter where a person might be.

Representation

When your child thinks of a particular thing, they might have one picture that comes to mind. For example, if they've had a negative experience with a dog, and you ask them to picture a dog, they might only picture that one vicious dog. With that picture, or that representation, they then only think of dogs as being mean. Changing the representations and introducing new pictures helps to create new reactions and new actions.

State

A child can have a number of different states they might experience in their lives. For example, they might be happy at some moments, sad at others. The state your child might be in right now may not be positive for them. With NLP, they can begin to create the state they want to have during their life.

Subconscious

The things we have experienced and learned in our lives create thoughts in our mind. Sometimes, these thoughts aren't clearly defined and we don't know where these thoughts or feelings come from. Going back to the angry dog, when a person has a bad experience with a dog in their life it is possible they will always fear dogs, even though they never had another negative experience. In fact, the person might not even remember the experience they had, but still have the subconscious thought that they need to get away from any dog they see.

There are other terms that will come up in relation to NLP, but the key is to focus on the results you see. If you find another word that works better for you, then use it.

Does NLP work for everyone?

Some parents may wonder if NLP works for everyone. After all, you might not want to spend your energy and time on something that might fail.

First of all, this is a frame that you are putting on your own experience of other tools or books you have read. While other books and tools might not have worked, there is no connection that NLP won't work for your child.

In fact, NLP is even more effective when you simply believe it will be. The power of positive thinking is something that is a true result of NLP and of the process of reprogramming thoughts. When a person follows the techniques and believes they will work, they will see results.

Changing the Way You Interact

The interactions you have with your child are where the learning process begins. From the way you talk to your child and the way you perceive your child, you are teaching them new things.

When you want to create a positive setting and life for your children, you need to look at the way you interact with them and you need to begin to understand there are things that can improve—let's be honest there is always scope to do something better.

Since you are always interacting in some way, these little changes will add up to big results, even if you don't see them immediately.

Positive perceptions

One of the best ways to begin to change the interactions you have with other people is to change your attitude. It makes sense to avoid statements about your child that are negative (although you know you never loved them any less while using such statements):
- They're up to something
- What have they done now?
- What's wrong now?

These statements, and others like them, contribute to the feeling in your child that they are "wrong". Let's rather start afresh.
Instead, you can focus on the good that is in your child and think of ways that you can create a positive environment through the words you choose, for example:
- What are you creating?
- What have they learned?
- What can be fixed?

- How can we be happy?

The more positive words you can build into your speech, the more your child will hear the words and take them to heart. Like anything else, these words will become thoughts. They will think of these words when they are with you and they will associate happiness and positive feelings when they are at home. Over time, your kids will be able to take these feelings and bring them into other environments, even if they are surrounded by people who choose not to create a more positive attitude or outlook.

A coaching attitude

While you might be thinking that being a teacher for your children is the best way to help them, there is an even better way you can create a connection with your child—by acting as their coach. This creates a dynamic of "we're in this together" rather than you being a person who tells them what to think and how to behave.

When you look at a coach of an athletic team, you will notice they are working with each team player to see how they can improve what they already know. They are talking with the players about what they could do better.

Instead of focusing on what went wrong (because things can't be changed when they already happened), the coach is a person who talks with the player and tries to help them understand what might be a better option the next time they're in a certain situation.
For example, if your child accidentally breaks a glass, you might approach the situation in this manner:
- What happened?
- What caused the glass to fall?
- How might you avoid this situation in the future?
- What can you do now to make this situation "better"?

As you can see, there is no accusatory language in this conversation. All you are doing is coaching the child to see what happened and how they could have avoided the issue.

And that's really all there is to it. Focus on how you can guide your child to the lessons they want to learn, and avoid putting words in their mouths or expecting a certain answer.

While you as an adult might expect your child to answer that they would avoid a repeat of the situation by not putting a glass on the edge of the table, their response could instead be that they won't use that certain glass again. Instead of correcting them, ask them: "What else…"

This will allow the child to see there are a number of different solutions for the issue, even if they don't realise it at first.

You can coach your child into learning what they need to learn, given the things that have happened in a certain situation. The more you can guide them to the answers they need, no matter what these are, the more they will be able to follow this process when something like this happens again.

Building rapport with your child

When you are working with your child to help them learn and to grow, it's a good idea to focus on building rapport with your child first. This will help them feel comfortable with you and to feel you are on their level. Think about how you feel with different people, and how some just seem to "get" you while others don't.

When you are with your child, you can create the same feeling. All you need to do is to build rapport first.
Start by looking at your child to see what kind of person they are. You may think you know everything about them there is to

know, but it's time to get to know them even better.
Look at how they act in their everyday lives:

- Do they get nervous about anything?
- How do they interact with siblings?
- What do they do when they are doing homework?
- How do they solve problems?
- How do they speak?
- How do they move their bodies?

Like a case study, look at your child from a somewhat more independent vantage point to see the details you might overlook on a daily basis. Learning who your child is allows you to start the foundation of strong rapport.

Mirroring

One of the easiest ways to begin to establish a stronger rapport with your child is to look at how they act and then try to act in the same way. This is known as "mirroring".

You can mirror someone by looking at the way they act and then copying it. Try this with a partner or with a friend first to see how it works. It might seem a little awkward at first, but you will notice the other person is much more comfortable with you as a result.

There are a number of things you can observe, and then try to mirror as much of it as you can. This includes:

- The way they stand
- The way they talk – the tone of voice and speed
- The words they choose
- The body positions
- The facial expressions

You can mirror a great many qualities in another person, allowing them to feel on a subconscious level that you are someone who understands them. They will feel at ease with you because they don't feel you are opposing them in any way.

Even if your words are not in complete agreement with them, they will still feel you understand them. The mind picks up on these subtle things, even if it doesn't seem like it could.

And when you practice this mirroring with your child, they too will begin to settle and feel as though you understand them on a deeper level.

Matching

Another way to build rapport with anyone, including your child, is to match what they are saying and how they are saying it. When you listen intently to your child, you will notice they say certain things or they repeat certain phrases.

If you can match these phrases, then you will create the sensation that you understand them and that you are someone who really knows who they are. In time, you might begin to steer the conversation, using the things you have heard as clues to how to talk to your child. This will allow you to teach them certain lessons, show them certain actions, and encourage them to behave in certain ways.
They are still going to be just as unique, but you will be someone that they can be unique with. Some good ways to match include:
- Using the same lengths of words
- Using the same number of words in a sentence
- Repeating phrases
- Focusing on simple matching of ideas
- Talking about the same subjects

The more practice you have with matching, the easier it will become. In time, you will also know how to talk to certain people, so you can switch on and off the way that you speak.

And each person will feel you understand them completely— this is something that is especially important when you have

more than one child.
Let your child set the pace.
When talking with your child, it can be challenging to talk at their pace. But when you do, your child will feel immediately comfortable and will settle into a calm conversation with you. If they're feeling rushed or they're feeling like you're talking too slowly for them, they will feel uncomfortable.

If you ever look at a conversation between yourself and your friends, you will notice that one person generally leads the conversation. No matter what you're talking about, one person is the starter of the conversation and they are often the loudest voice during the whole conversation.

Those who don't talk as loudly or at the same pace as this person often feel left out. But when everyone is at the same energy level as that person, everyone feels included and everyone feels like they are creating a productive conversation. Let your child set the pace of your conversations in order to help them feel as though you understand them and that you're able to meet them at their pace. In time, their pace might change, but it's not up to you to change it. They will fall into a natural rhythm with you if you begin to allow for their pace to do what it needs to do.

Naturally, your child will begin to mirror your pace too and you will both begin to feel more comfortable as a result.

Practicing rapport

You can practice rapport any time you like, but it's best to practice with a friend first to see what their reaction is. Don't tell them straight up that you are doing this, but once you feel that you have practiced enough you can ask them what they felt when you were acting in a certain way.

For example, you might want to talk with a friend about a certain event you want to plan and then use rapport-building techniques to see if they agree with you more than they normally would. Afterwards let them know what you did to see how it impacted them.

Once you are comfortable, you may want to try this same sort of practice with your child when you speak with them. You don't have to have a goal in mind during a conversation, just try mirroring and matching to see if it changes the way you relate with your child.

Many people will notice they are able to have better conversations with their children and that their children are more attentive as a result of having better rapport.

Your child's eye movements[37]

One of the more controversial ways you can connect with your child and help them begin to see what they need is to learn about eye movements. While you might not be aware of it, when you think about something your eyes can move in a particular direction, in order to access a certain piece of information.What does this mean?

When you see your child move their eyes in a certain direction, you might be able to see patterns in the way they think. Here are some of the common patterns you might notice in your child (but please remember not all children or people are the same):

- Eyes move up and to the right: Creating mental pictures
- Eyes move up and to the left: Remembering mental pictures
- Eyes move to the right: Creating sounds
- Eyes move to the left: Remembering sounds
- Eyes move down and to the right: Touch, smell, emotions and tastes
- Eyes move down and to the left: Listening to internal chatter

You can actually find out what your child might do when they are accessing certain kinds of information by asking of them questions. By keeping track of where their eyes move, you will begin to see how they are learning and remembering.

What is the point of this?
This information provides you with clues when you are talking to your child about how to direct the conversation. For example, if you notice a child is looking down and to the left, you might ask them if they have something on their mind they'd like to share.

The more you can become attuned with your child, the more you will be able to help them learn and the more you will be able to help them grow.

Focus on what you do want

The main key to making sure your child has the support they need to be happy and healthy is to focus on what you want from them.

Focusing on what you want creates a frame in your own mind that is focused on the idea your child is going to succeed. When you put your energy toward what you want, you also allow your child a chance to focus on what they can do to reach these ideas you believe about them.

For example, if you focus on how your child easily completes their homework, they are going to hear this language and believe it as well. Soon enough they will sit down to homework and think that everything is easy for them. They won't even have to talk themselves into it, it will just become second nature.

And if you use some of the rapport building tools above, you can talk to your child about how easy it is for them to do their homework in a positive and effective manner. As a result they will be more comfortable with the ideas you are introducing to them, and they will begin to take in this information.

What do you want?

When you're working with your child and trying to help them succeed in life, you need to have a clear understanding of what you want. But if you're not sure how your child might be able to progress, doesn't this become tricky?

That's an excellent point.
Since not all NLP techniques will work in quite the same way as they do for different people, you need to create a list of general goals that you want to achieve from the NLP work you and your child will do together.

No matter what you do, you will see some reward. But more than anything it is the goals that you set that will motivate, inspire and encourage.Even when things don't seem to be moving as quickly as you'd like, the goals that you do set with your child will help

keep them on the path, using the tools they will learn in this book.Here are some ways to think about with your child what you want to achieve from NLP work together.

First things first, delete these words from your vocabulary (and when you learn how to, please let me know):
- Should
- Must
- Have to
- Mustn't
- Can't
- Got to

If you use these words and phrases in goals, you are creating the idea in your brain that it might not be possible. While this is certainly always the case, if you want to project success, you need to think in words that support success.

When you set goals for your NLP work, you need to focus on:
- Goals for success
- Flexibility
- Patience

More specific NLP-related goals might include:
- Better behaviour
- Increased school performance
- Less stress in the household
- Improved learning
- Positive interactions with others

This list can be more extensive, but with NLP, all of these ideas can be addressed and they can be achieved. By having a clear direction in which you want to travel with your child, you will begin to create a positive statement and intention for your NLP practices.

You will know the outcomes of your practices will be positive and that your goals are helpful to all in the family.
If your child is interested, it is a good idea to create this set of goals with them. Many children are just as frustrated with their experiences as you might be. They might feel overwhelmed about learning or about their relationships to others in their lives.

They need you to help them begin to function more positively and more effectively. When this can happen as a collaborative effort, you can both celebrate the results and enjoy them.

Of course, as you begin to work toward these goals, you might find they need to change or they need to be altered. Part of being a positive role model and aid in the development of your child is to make sure you are flexible.

Even though you might have two children, they don't learn the same way and the NLP techniques may need to be adjusted to suit each of their needs. This is a good thing.

Learning to be flexible also creates the idea for your children that being flexible is a good thing. They will learn to appreciate the differences in others and they will learn it is possible to work with those differences, as opposed to fighting them.

Finally, and this is a lesson we can all learn more about, patience is the key to any process that involves your child and in changing the way they work in the world.

Not everyone is going to have immediate results and not everyone is going to be able to reach every single goal right away. There may be times when you fall back into old patterns or your child starts following old habits. These aren't times of failure—they're times where you can learn how to become an even better teacher, parent and role model.

Your child might also need time to incorporate the new ideas and patterns into their minds. When this happens, you need to be patient as they will eventually "get" it, but it may take a little while.

When your kids see you exercising your patience, it also allows them to be more patient with themselves too. They will understand that their learning may take as long as it takes. Besides, it's not a contest anyway, is it?

Goal-Setting Steps

Here is a nine-step process you use in order to create goals that are attainable, congruent, and positive.

Step #1 – What do you want?

This question is probably seared in your mind at this point. What do you want from this book, from this process and from this work?

State the goals of your NLP work with your child in a positive way, for example:
- My child behaves appropriately
- My child's grades are A's
- My child's communication is positive
- My child is calm and organised

No matter what the goals are that you create, choose to phrase them in a way that supports them already happening and already being a part of your existence.

This will ensure your brain is focused on success as you help your child along the way.

Step # 2 – What's going on?

Right now, think about what's happening with your child that has led to the creation of the goals. Are there specific instances that have led to the need for NLP?

Or are you interested in this work with your child in order to prevent future issues? Think about what's going on right now and talk about it in the first person perspective (that is your perspective) as though it is happening in the present day.

For example:
- I am frustrated
- I am feeling stuck
- When you do that I feel

Naming what is happening right now might seem to give importance to it, but it's simply creating a clear definition of the "now" in order to compare it to the future when that emerges.

Step #3 – What is the end result?

How will you know when you have achieved your goal? When you're working with your child, it is important to know what the end result will look like. By doing this, you will both know when you get there.

It's a good idea to describe what the eventual outcome will be, in the present tense, talking about the different things that will make up this moment:
- What does it feel like?
- What does it sound like?
- What does it look like?
- What will the home look like?

Ask yourself what the world will be like when you have reached the certain goals you have in mind.

Step #4 – What will the outcome provide?

As a result of the process of using NLP to reach certain goals, what are you able to see in order to know that you have been successful?

Choosing just one or two signs to watch out for can help you to create a clear understanding of when you arrive "there" as opposed to it being some nebulous future.

What are you able to do as a result of implementing and teaching the NLP? What are you able to do as a parent when you and your child are using these techniques together?

Will this result be congruent with the goals you have for your family and will the results be able to work within the family rules as well?

Step #5 – Are you responsible for the result?

The answer to this question is actually simple—yes. If you aren't responsible for helping your child, then you should not be practicing NLP techniques with them as that might step on some toes.

A teacher is in a position where they are able to impact a child and they have the permission to do so. But if you're not given the responsibility of helping a child, you are not responsible for the result of the NLP. In that instance, it is better to step back from the situation.

Step #6 – What is the context?

While you might feel the context for the goals you want to meet with your child is at home, this is not the only place where these NLP practices might be used. They can also be applied at school, at the babysitter's house, a relative's home or any public setting.

Think about where you would want your child to use the skills you are teaching them with the NLP work you will be doing. Where, how, when, and with whom do you want your child to be practicing and using NLP practices?

Step #7 – What do you need?

As a parent, you might feel your resources are limited, but this is far from true. When you are working with NLP and you want to try something, but you're not sure how, what resources do you have to turn to?

Creating a list of the possible books or study guides you can use will allow you to turn to these points of reference when needed. And if you don't need the resources, at least you have them readily available.

Step # 8 – Who can help you?

Ideally, seek someone out who can help you with your child's needs. This might be a person who is training others in NLP or it might be someone who is interested in child development.

Seek out experts in your local area who are available for questions and for advice. You will likely find that people are happy to help you when it comes to the support of your child.

This a very serious question to ask yourself. What will happen to your home if the NLP practices aren't effective? When you stop to consider this, you can see just how important it is to maintain your practices and exercises as much as possible.

You might motivate yourself with the goals you have in place, but also with the reality of what might happen if goals aren't met.

(But don't focus your energy here. Instead, focus on what you will gain from using NLP).

The end goal

The end goal of your work with your child is simple: To create the ideal conditions in which they can be happy and you can be happy too.

By creating clear communication between you and your child, you allow the both of you to gain positive experiences from your time together, and this adds up to a kid who is able to enjoy the world.

They will feel understood, valued, and confident. What other reasons are more important than that?

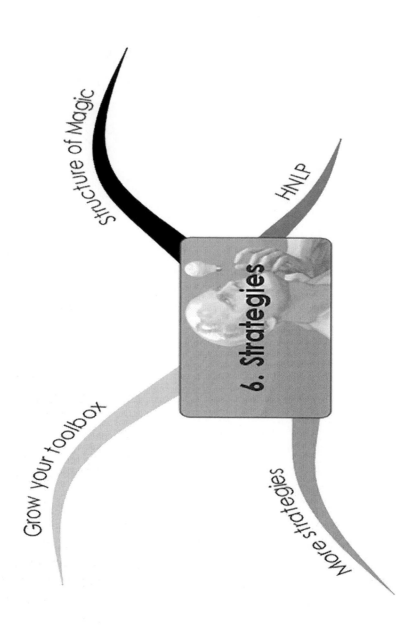

Structure of Magic

HNLP

Grow your toolbox

More strategies

6. Strategies

Chapter 6
NLP Strategies

"And above all, watch with glittering eyes the whole world around you because the greatest secrets are always hidden in the most unlikely places. Those who don't believe in magic will never find it."

Roald Dahl

The Structure of Magic

When my client Mr. Watson, a school headmaster, asked me if I could "work some magic" on a six-year old student who had a terrible stammer, I smiled and said, "Of course." To be quite honest I hadn't a clue but I felt confident that the little chap had all the resources inside of him to speak without his stammer.

I had been working with young children for a few years in private practice by then, and Mr. Watson had retained my services, on an ad hoc basis, to support any children in his school with behavioural problems. There was a lot of red tape as usual, but Mr. Watson always looked out for the child's interests above anything else, and would do what he needed to do to enable me to work with his pupil.

The day arrived and I was invited into Mr. Watson's office. Mr. Watson then left and collected little Jimmy from his class. I'd like you to keep in mind that Jimmy, was, on an unconscious level, utilising his stammer to capture more attention, mostly from his parents and the world at large. This meant Jimmy would need a new strategy to help him to move beyond this developmental stage.

While I was alone in the office, I sat in Mr. Watson's chair so that when the two of them came back, they would have to sit on the other side of the desk.

Mr. Watson looked very puzzled as he walked in and sat down on the wrong side of the powerful desk. He said nothing other than to introduce Jimmy to "Mr. Hudson".

Jimmy was a freckled-faced, ginger-haired, young boy. "Do you like Bart Simpson?" I asked. Jimmy looked puzzled, so I repeated the question, adding that Bart was "my favorite character." Jimmy smiled and nodded in total bemusement.

I then went on to explain that, while watching an episode a few days earlier, the show began to run "out of sync". Suddenly, Bart's mouth was moving but Homer was speaking. "It's frustrating, isn't it?" I said to a now curious Jimmy.

The young boy stared back at me with a knowing look on his face.

"Then everything has to STOP, Jimmy!" I said with a downward inflection in my voice. "And when everything is STOPPED, Jimmy, then everything can be realigned so that everybody is speaking with their own voice. Now, isn't that interesting?" Before Jimmy had a chance to respond, I dismissed him with, "You can go back to your classroom now, Jimmy; thank you."

As a bewildered Jimmy left the headmaster's office, an equally bewildered Mr. Watson sat staring at me, clearly wondering what had just gone on.

"Matt," he said, in his Edinburgh twang. "You can't expect me to cough up for that?" I took that to mean he didn't want to pay for my latest "performance". I remember mentioning to him that I was feeling a little like the Pied Piper after ridding Hamlin of its rats; the people of the village that had been plagued by the pests were suddenly unwilling to pay now that the problem was gone and the piper had rid them of the rats!

The headmaster raised an eyebrow and looked at me, his face filled with doubt and disbelief. I smiled at Mr. Watson knowingly, enjoying the view from behind his big wooden desk. "Trust me on this one Phil," I said.

"All right!" he said, extending his faith in me, at least for now. Then he chuckled, "Can I at least have my bloody chair back, now?"

The next day Mr. Watson rang me to say that Jimmy's mum and dad were at the school and little Jimmy had woken up without his stammer.

"How the blooming heck did you do it?" asked a now fully-trusting, amazed although still confused Mr. Watson. "Elementary, my dear Watson," I replied wryly.

What I did was to utilise all of the information that you have been given in this book and many years' experience. Let me explain in a little more detail: Jimmy had a limiting belief about being a "stammerer". In other words, his identity was connected to this habit. To see better how I accomplished this goal, let's have a look at the session from Jimmy's side of the desk.

Question: When does a child go to the headmaster's office?

Answer: When you've been really good – or when you've been really bad.
The head teacher is usually behind his large, imposing desk. So, if there is someone else sitting in the head's chair, and Mr. Watson doesn't tell him to move, not only that, he just sits quietly on the "wrong" side of the desk alongside Jimmy, then that person must have more power than the headmaster.

Step 1
Associating Jimmy in his present or problem state
This "powerful" person likes The Simpsons, just like me.

Step 2
Dissociate Jimmy from his problem
From Jimmy's perspective, the person behind the desk gets frustrated, just like him. "If I haven't been bad, then this person must have something… good… for me?" he thinks.

Step 3
Discovering Jimmy's resources and associating him to the resources.
In other words The Simpsons and Bart in particular.

Step 4
I have Jimmy associate his resources to the problem. By telling him that everything must stop before they can recover from being out of sync.

All of the above are positive beliefs. Now, by not allowing Jimmy to talk, I prevented him from identifying himself to me as a "Stammerer". Then, by dismissing him without explanation, I maintained his confusion while still feeling good about himself.
Finally…

Step 5
Future pacing Jimmy's resources, I had seeded a strategy for Jimmy to let go of his stammer. This way Jimmy would be puzzling over our conversation all day long and as he sailed into sleep that night, everything would STOP for Jimmy. The next day Jimmy had stopped and then started again—without his stammer.

Yes, there is a method hidden in my madness and more often than not as Milton Erickson, an American psychiatrist who specialised in medical hypnosis, would put it: "Any explanation is a therapeutic mistake."

What Erickson meant by this statement, is that the client already has all the answers they need to resolve their issue; as therapists, we just have to find a way to propel our clients above and beyond their current definition of themselves, outside the boundary of their self-limiting beliefs and into chaos and confusion. It is in that confusion that they are able to tap into the infinite possibilities that are there for all of us if we do but dare to take that step and transcend the threshold of our self-imposed "safe house".

Remember: "Confusion is the step before enlightenment." So don't be afraid to be confused; it's the first step to eliminating your limiting self-beliefs.

Perhaps, it's worth noting that although most parents won't be able to perform this level of "magic" immediately, the case study serves to remind you how powerful the mind is, and what a huge role you can play in helping your children overcome their self-limitations and obstacles.[38]

The Mother of All NLP Patterns

A wonderful man by the name of John Overdurf pointed out the process that underpins NLP patterns.[39] He calls it the "Mother of all NLP" and it works.

Basically you follow the five steps below within your interaction with your child and change is possible, even for a novice:
1. Associate the child to the problem
2. Dissociate the child from the problem
3. Discover the child's Resources and Associate the child to them
4. Associate Resources to the Problem
5. Future Pace Resources

It was thanks to John and Julie Silverthorn that Humanistic Neuro-Linguistic Psychology (HNLP) came into being. That is what my wife, Sonya Hudson, and friends Henk and Carla Beljaars teach today.

NLP Techniques You Can Use

When you're ready to add NLP practices to your child's life, it's time to look at all of the possibilities and practices that impact children most effectively.

Truthfully, there are many hundreds of NLP patterns you can use to create a positive life for you and for your child, but when you want to create the most change in your child, it's better to focus on practices that will impact their age level.

In this section, you will learn about four basic NLP practices, how to use them, and how to ensure they impact your child positively.

Anchoring

What you might not realise is that everyone uses anchors— every day, in fact. While you might not realise that you're doing it or that you have done it in the past, it's something we do unconsciously in order to relate to our environment.

Remember a time when you were a child and you got sick after eating a certain food like a dodgy fish pie? You might not like eating that food today because of that association, and because you remember a certain emotional state that was connected to it. And feeling really ill wasn't a good connection to make.

Though you might have been sick anyway, or it was a unique occurrence, the connection that you make in your brain can be so strong that you might not be able to break it as easily as you made it. That's anchoring.

When you can create a new anchor for your child, you can begin to create a new feeling for them in their life. If there are certain situations that cause them to feel anxious, for example, you can help them create anchors that allow them to feel calm.

Right now, stop and think about a great day in your life. Think about a time when you were happy and calm and you felt that nothing could be more perfect. This might be a holiday, a certain day, or some other event in your life.

It doesn't matter what the event is, but it matters what the feeling is. You need to create as strong a feeling as possible—and hold onto it.When you look around your mind during this experience, think about what is in the room with you. Think about one thing in this memory that takes you instantly back to that feeling.

For example, if you are thinking about a wedding, you might think of the ring that you have on your finger as something that brings you back to that day. That is the anchor. When you look at that ring again, you can bring yourself back to the experience, even though you can't live that experience again.

You can develop similar anchors with your kids.
But you might have noticed that when you look at the anchor again, you don't feel 100% as happy as you did at the time of the actual memory. That's okay. Even though you might not feel the exact feelings, you will begin to connect those emotions to the anchor. This will help you call back those emotions whenever you call back the anchor.

You might:
- Carry a symbol of an anchor with you
- Close your eyes and remember the memory or the anchor when you need to
- Have a picture in your office or home to remind you of this anchor

All of these techniques can help you and your child begin to create a strong anchor to a feeling they want to access during their days.

Since children learn in different ways, it's a good idea to try out different anchor systems so that you can find one that works best for your child. Or they might want to have an anchor for all of these sorts of learning.

This will prepare them to have an easier time learning the information, no matter how it is being taught to them in a classroom or by you.

Auditory

Some children are more focused on learning in an auditory way through the sounds they hear. If your child seems to connect more with this sort of learning, they will respond better to auditory cues and anchors.

You can have certain anchors in place in your home when your kids are doing things that make them happy. For example, if they are practicing their favourite dance, you might want to play certain music. Other ways to make sure your child anchors into a positive emotional state is to have other anchors at hand like white noise machines, classical music, a bell to get their attention and certain music albums.

Either way, to create an effective anchor you need to make sure you connect positive feelings to these sounds. Also, choose sounds your child already likes since that will further boost the effectiveness of this anchor. Here are some ideas for anchoring the sounds for your child:

Tell them a story where they are the hero

When you are with your child, either before bed or at another time, have them close their eyes and tell them a story where they do everything right and they are the hero that wins. At the same time, use certain sounds again and again to help anchor that sound with the feeling of being a hero and of being confident.

Use certain music to wake up to

If your child has troubles waking up, it's a good idea to play the same sort of music in the morning as you begin a more positive routine. The more you do this, the more your child will begin to associate good things with the morning.

Use music in everyday settings

Whenever you are with your child, associate positive activities with music. Use music in the car on the way to school, for example, as you talk about how wonderful their day is going to be. This will connect positive goals with the music.

When frustrated, try something new

If you notice your child is getting frustrated or is having troubles when they are using certain anchors, talk with them about something else. They will probably be able to suggest another anchor that will work even better for them.

Sit down with your child and ask them what sounds they like to hear during the day. Or you might simply want to watch your child over the course of a few weeks to see what they turn to when they are upset or when they want to cheer themselves up. They might already be telling you what anchors will be the best fit for their needs.

Kinesthetic

When you have a child who tends to respond to experiences more than they do to auditory cues and anchors, you will need to create different kinds of anchors.

These anchors work well for children who tend to get their hands into everything, or who just can't seem to sit still. And although these NLP practices are simpler than having your kid run around the room to expend extra energy, they are no less effective.

Create some sort of physical touch which grounds them back into a positive mental state. Since they can't run around the classroom in order to access this state, they will need to choose another sensation.

This sensation might be connected to a movement they did when they felt positive and happy. For example, if your child is into sports, you might want to ask them about their favourite game memory. What were they doing? If they were playing baseball and they were up at the plate, ask them how they held their hands around the bat. Just returning to that simple movement can create positive feelings for them.

Other ideas include:
- Having your child wear a favourite outfit
- Setting up a comfortable space for homework
- Creating a connection between a hand position and a positive emotion

When your child is nervous about something that is happening in their life, it's a good idea to encourage them to think back to that happy event they held in their mind before.
Have them focus on it hard and then have them touch their pointer finger to their thumb, creating a little circle. While they're still thinking about the happiness and joy of the memory, they can remember the touch they have anchored

along with the emotions. This is a great practice and one that can be used again and again for any number of situations.

You can also ask your child to think of a time when they were really calm, patient or happy. By bringing your child to that state and then having them touch a part of their body where they can anchor that feeling, they can always go back to touch that point when they need to be soothed. Of course, lucky socks don't hurt either.

Visual

When your child is more focused on visual cues for their learning and for their emotional states, you will need to create a few visual anchors that can help them return to happiness.

Visual learners might want to have reminders of their happy memories in the environment around them, for example:

Hang pictures of happy memories

If your child has a certain event they connect to positive emotions, you can to surround them with the positive visual cues from this memory. These pictures should be hanging in their study area or in their bedroom to make them feel calm.

Add pictures to school notebooks

You can also tape these pictures onto schoolbook covers and notebooks to help your child always be around visual cues for happiness and confidence.

Have souvenirs to look at

Having actual items from memorable vacations or other memories can also help a child remember these memories and hang onto their emotions.

Encourage positive emotions with certain people

If your child has a positive memory of a person, or they can recall one, it can help them when they are in certain situations. For example, if a child is having troubles in a class, they might want to remember a fun memory of their teacher to help enhance their learning process.

Think about symbols to use

You might also want to create symbols that can be a part of your child's life to anchor in a certain emotion. For example, a child might like the peace sign symbol so make sure that symbol is up in different places. It might be a part of their bedroom, but it can also be a part of their schoolbooks.

Visual cues are easy to add to a space. If and when these cues become less effective, you can change them to something new, based on the new experiences of your child.

Language

Just as there are different ways in which children anchor to certain emotions, there are different language systems that will work better for them when they are in the home and in the classroom.

This system is just as you would expect:
- Auditory
- Inner Dialogue
- Kinesthetic
- Visual

When you are speaking with your child, you need to learn to speak their language. By doing this, they will feel understood, heard, and they will begin to create a better emotional state for themselves. They will not feel they have to fight with communication.

To learn what sort of language your child might want to talk in and be talked to in, here are a few samples of the different words a child might use when they are in one of the four language systems above.

Auditory	Inner Dialogue	Kinesthetic	Visual
Speak	Sense	Feel	See
Call	Think	Grasp	Picture
Hear	Learn	Touch	Bright
Listen	Process	Pull	Colourful
Yell	Consider	Numb	Shining

If you want to see what these different styles look like in practice, here is an example for a child who feels his teacher doesn't listen to him.

Auditory: My teacher goes deaf whenever I speak up
Kinesthetic: I feel like my teacher doesn't get me
Visual: My teacher doesn't see me sitting in the classroom

What's happening is that different people are using different ways of explaining the same thing because they experience and represent the world around them in different ways. When you begin to realise what your child understands and what they need to hear in order to learn, you can begin to adjust your dialogue to be more helpful and supportive of their needs.

They may not realise they are choosing certain words, but they can begin to see that you are listening to them and responding in a way that makes them feel heard and that makes them feel as though you aren't just nodding your head when they speak.

So how do you actually use this knowledge in your everyday life?

Listen to your child speak

Take some time to really listen to what your child says and what words they use. While they might use words from all of these categories, it's most likely they will use more words from one category than another.

Try to match the way they speak

If your child talks about how they can't see what's happening, tell them that you will show them what's happening.

The more you practice, the easier it will get

You need to practice, just as your child will need to practice in order to learn more about how to use NLP. Be ready to practice what you need to say in order to function at the same language level as your child.

The more you see the patterns in the way your child speaks, the better your rapport will be. Your child will feel you hear them and they will feel more comfortable about expressing themselves.

This will help you both become better at communicating, and will help your child when they are in school. They will also learn how to communicate more effectively with others.

Metaphor

The first thing you might have thought when you read the title of this section is that it's too hard for a child to understand the idea of metaphors. After all, many adults don't understand them.

Keep in mind that children tend to understand things on different levels than adults. Sometimes, not thinking too hard about something makes it easier to understand. Besides, we use metaphors all the time.

Think about the last time you needed to explain something to someone, but it wasn't something that was concrete. For example, when you had to tell someone about a trip you took to a new place and the other person had never been there.

You could describe the place you went to, but you might also have described the actual traveling in metaphor.
- Took the long road
- Traveling through mud
- The back way

All of these phrases aren't literal, they're figurative. And while they might seem clear to you, they are not always clear to the person who is listening. This is why metaphors are so helpful, actually, even though they sound like they would be anything but helpful.

What you need to remember is that kids sometimes process information in different ways than adults. While you might be able to understand the idea your child is trying to share, you might have more troubles figuring out what it means to them. Enter metaphor. Just as when you were looking at the language that someone uses to determine what sort of words they need to hear in response, metaphors can reveal a lot about a person.

When a person talks about homework as being a foggy mess. They're talking about visual cues and they are describing the homework as being messy. When you respond to them, you might want to ask them what might help them to see the answers better. As you may have noticed, the metaphors offer clues into the way the child is thinking. But you need to listen carefully in order to know how to respond to this information.

Whenever you begin to hear a child talk about something in terms of a metaphor, you can encourage them to tell you more. This will help you get an even better sense of what is going on. When they need to tell someone more, they will have to think harder on what they have just said and how it really can be described to someone else.

Here are some ways you can begin to use the idea of metaphors in your communication with your child:

Think like a child

Stop thinking about things in terms of literal words and descriptions. Instead of thinking about a zoo, for example, like a building with a lot of different animals in it, think about how you might describe the zoo from the point of view of a lion.

Ask your child for a story or poem

When you want to talk to your child about something, ask them to tell you a story about what is happening for them. They will be able to give you clues in metaphors that will help you better understand what you need to know about them. When you talk with your child, what you are doing is creating a story that will help you to understand the road their brain takes when it is moving from point A to point B.

The more that you understand how their brain moves, the easier it will be to follow. This process is called constructing a narrative. Children are the heroes of their own story. While you might not hear their story all the time, you might hear snippets of their own inner dialogue.

For example, if your child has a lot of troubles with the idea of math, they might call their math homework "the enemy". When you know they are creating a name for their homework, you can talk to them about their problems at this level.

Instead of talking to them about math as a subject they have in school, you can ask them what weapons they need to slay their enemy. While it might seem like metaphors are a way of making this more abstract, they're actually ways to create narratives that are more enjoyable to the child. Within each story a child creates, they can reveal everything from emotions and spiritual beliefs to personal values and troubles with friends.

No matter what you might think about a story that seems to be going nowhere for your child, it always means something. In order to utilise metaphor with your child in a positive way, help them to construct personal metaphors about different areas of their lives.

You can do this by:

Asking them for more details

Even when they appear to be finished telling the story, ask for more details. This will help you be sure you are getting all of the details related to that matter.

Repeating their story to them

Repeat their story back to them, using their words as much as possible.

Relating a solution in their own words

If they seem to need a solution, ask them questions about it in a way that will help them see the solution on their own or come to a new solution that works for them.

Rewording the story in another way

If the narrative is talking about the idea that the child is lost in the woods, then you might want to talk to them about the fact that they have a ladder in their pocket and they can put it down, climb up, and eventually see over the trees to find their way out.

Using their language at a later time

If there is a word or a phrase they use in their story that holds a lot of emotion for them, make sure you use it again when you talk with your child.

Here is an example of a story a child might tell: When I do my English homework, I begin to go into a freak out. I don't know what to do and I'm just lost in the woods without anywhere to go. I try to look at the words, but they blur together and I can't see what they mean. And in my freak out, I can't think straight enough to come up with an answer to the questions or to write my paper. It just stinks and I think that I'm stupid.

When you hear a story like this you can notice one thing that was repeated a few times—freak out. This phrase doesn't mean anything to you, but it means a lot to the child. If the child is having troubles at a later time, a parent might want to ask if they are having a freak out.

What's great about the idea of a metaphor is that it takes the burden off your child's shoulders. They aren't the ones with the troubles, the problem is the one with the problem. Let's explore this a little more...

Going back to the freak out, you will notice the child didn't talk about how bad they are. They started to at the end, but if you, as the parent, turned the conversation into a conversation about how to deal with the freak out, then the child wouldn't feel there was anything wrong with them. Here are some tips to use metaphors to calm your child and help them become their own problem solvers:

Have the child describe it

Have your child talk about the problem and begin to describe it. This will help you better understand what the child sees when they are faced with this problem.

Use that word when talking about the problem

If there is a word or a name associated with the problem, you should use that name when talking to your kid.

Consider a new word if the child doesn't have one

If the child doesn't already have a name for the problem, try to come up with one together. This will help to externalise the issue and it will make it more controllable.

Talk about the word, not the child

Whenever the problem comes up again, talk about the problem, not about the child as the problem. When you allow the child to be separate, they will be much more likely to solve the problem.

At first it may be hard to notice when your child, or yourself, turn to metaphor. But the more you notice your child talking in metaphor, the more you can use this to help them begin to sort out their troubles in a positive way.

No matter what they might be feeling, there is a way to describe it. And once you've described it, you can start to tame it.

Reframing

Reframing is the process by which we change or transform meanings.

A simple reframe Matt's mother often used with him when he was a boy and whimpered about how he had lost something, she would say: "You mean misplaced." That reframe still works for him and makes him smile to this day. You see, the past is the past, it is done, but how you think about it is very much alive and kicking, so you can teach your child how to learn from experience and grow or how to cling to an impoverished reality that serves no one.

The basic presuppositions of reframing are:
1. Every experience in the world and every behaviour is appropriate given some context, some frame
2. Reframing changes the individual's internal context
3. The behaviours, which are the most challenging to work with, occur when the majority of the client's context is internal

There are two types of reframing:

1. **Context:** "too," "more," "less," (comparative deletion or generalisation)

To reframe

Hold the behaviour constant and change context. Ask yourself: "In what context would this particular behaviour have value?"

For example

Because he considers carefully where every toy needs to be stored, your child takes far longer to tidy his bedroom than you would like. In this instance you can ask yourself where such behaviour could have value and may find your child's analytical nature really lends itself to detailed crafts and art.

2. **Meaning:** Verbs of causation: "is", "means"

A causes B: cause and effect
A means B: complex equivalence

To reframe

Hold context constant and change meaning of behaviour. *"What other positive value or meaning could this behaviour have?"*

When you think about your life, what frame do you use? Do you look at your life as a series of problems or a series of solutions? Do you think about your life the way your parents told you to think about it or do you think of your life in terms of what your partner tells you about it? These are all frames.

Just as there are rose-coloured spectacles through which you can view the world, there are spectacles of every possible colour. And each one creates a slightly different way of looking at your life.

Your child has the same sort of framing to manage.
Before you begin to create a new attitude of reframing, it is
key to understand that framing is a way a person limits
themselves in their lives.

Think about watching a movie on a television screen. You can
only see the picture that is within the screen, you can't see
anything beyond the screen itself.

If you're watching a widescreen movie, then you will see the
bars at the top and the bottom. Though you can't see those
spaces, the aspects are adjusted so you can see more of the
side-to-side image.

You can choose the frame you want to use. Do you want to
see more? Do you want to see less? Do you want to see
positive things in your life? Do you want to think the best of
people – or the worst?

You decide.
Framing can come from a number of different sources
including:
  • What a teacher says
  • What a parent says
  • What friends say
  • What the programmes on TV convey

A child will look at their world in a certain way if they have
been taught that a certain way is the way they should look at it.
But, this does not mean their framing needs to stay in place.

They can begin to change the way they perceive the world, with your help. Here is a series of questions a child should ask when they enter any situation:
- What is happening?
- What is the positive aspect of this situation?
- What is a positive meaning for the behaviour?

When you and your child begin to look at the world as only having positive purposes and results, you will begin to see that the world is not scary or difficult. Every day is filled with possibilities when you begin to look at it as though it has nothing but possibilities to offer.

You can teach your child some lessons that will help them continue to reframe their life in a meaningful and positive way:
- Every behaviour has a positive intention
- Every action can have a positive result
- Every person can have a positive attitude

Now, this isn't to say all your child just has to do is believe in the good in the world and they will always see it. If only things were that simple. What it will teach your child, however, is to consider that everyone has the best of intentions. This will allow a kid to be more open and more caring about the world around them.

They will not automatically assume the math test is going to be hard. They will walk into the room and think about how they have prepared as well as they could have. Here are a few other ways your child can learn to reframe their lives:
- Think about the best possible circumstance
- Think about the best possible motivation
- Think about the best possible result

When your child learns to believe in how successful they will be (not can be), they will see success in their lives. They will make choices that lead to success and they will understand that they are going to do the best they can, no matter where they are. It's time to put on the rose-coloured glasses, and never take them off again.

Some final exercises for you to use with your child in order to help them with reframing and with your own reframing:

Reframe out loud

At first, you can do your reframing out loud when you are with your child. This will help them to see what you are doing and how they can do it too.

Ask your child to reframe a difficult situation

Once your child has seen a few instances of reframing, ask them to step in and begin to say what they think is going on in a positive way.

Encourage reframing in conversations

When you are talking with your child, try to reframe what they are saying in a non-corrective way. This will help them to see they could think of things in a new way.
Whenever your child reframes a situation, be sure to let them know how proud you are of them. This will encourage them to continue with the reframing they have done and want to continue to do.

"Magic comes from what is inside you. It is a part of you. You can't weave together a spell that you don't believe in."

Jim Butcher

Additional NLP Exercises to Use

There are hundreds of NLP exercises you can use to help
your child improve their life and their attitude in life. You can
choose to use just a few of the basic ones that have already
been listed above, or you can continuously look for new
lessons that will help you and your child get the most from life.

This section will provide you with more NLP exercises that are
designed to help you help your child.

The alphabet game

This game was developed to help those who are kinesthetic
learners, and allows children to learn how to use both halves
of their brain.

You will need to create a chart that looks like this on the
ground:

A	B	C	D	E
L	T	R	T	L
F	G	H	I	J
L	R	L	T	R
K	L	M	N	O
L	R	T	R	T
P	Q	R	S	T
L	T	L	R	L
U	V	W	X	Y
T	L	T	R	R
Z				
T				

The grid letters are ALL CAPS alphabet letters:

R, L and T are the movement instructions for the child to
follow while reciting the alphabet:

R– Right hand goes up to shoulder level
L– Left hand goes up to shoulder level
T– Both hands go up to shoulder level while child jumps.

Once you have this grid in place, you need to have your child follow a certain set of instructions. Make sure the letters are large enough so your child can easily read them and see them as they are moving around.

Here are the steps:
- Have your child think about a problem they are facing and imagine a circle where they are standing, with the problem.
- Ask your child to step out of the circle and leave their problem in the circle.
- Instruct your child to call out the letters of the alphabet whilst raising their arms up and down. (In accordance with the diagram above)
- When your child has successfully completed three rounds of the game, without a trip or a fault, have them jump back onto their imaginary circle and notice what has changed in their problem.

The more the child is able to do this, the more they are syncing their right brain with their left brain and the more they will be able to bring a good state of mind to problems. Remember resilience is key.

They can also make the game more challenging by switching up the lowercase letters. Or adding in a one legged jump.

When both sides of the brain are involved in the processing of problems, the child will be able to accomplish more and they will be able to create more creative solutions.

The walking way

A simple way that will help a child begin to re-establish the way they think and react to a certain situation is walking. This process allows a child that is more kinesthetic to help create a connection between a certain behaviour and how they might react in a new and more effective way.

Here's what you will do:
- Think about a behaviour that needs to be changed. This is not something that you need to tell the child at this moment.
- Have your child walk back and forth or in some other predetermined pattern. This can be anything that is simple for them to remember and simple for them to repeat again and again.
- Have your child continue this pattern for a while until they are doing it without thinking about it.
- Once your child is walking, begin to suggest changes to the way they walk that will be more effective. Allow them to walk in a way that makes them feel more confident and powerful.
- Wait until they have established this new pattern and allow them to become comfortable in the mastery of this walk.
- When they are comfortable, begin to talk about the situation you have already predetermined – i.e. how to act when they're in a certain situation.
- As they think about this situation, encourage them to continue the walk, adjusting the way they move until they are back to walking with power and with grace.
- When the child is able to walk with power and grace while thinking about the situation...
- Talk about the situation again and see if their walk changes.
- If it does not, stop the exercise.

You can use this exercise with any sort of behaviour that you feel needs to be changed.

You can create a new walking pattern if you like, though it might be better to focus on the same powerful walk as this will help them to continue to create a connection of power.

They can then return to this walk when they need to work through a problem on their own or in the presence of you. This is a process that is also seen in other activities. For example when a child is good at a particular sport, they might feel powerful. In order to return to that powerful state, they can return to that sort of movement.

For example, they might go out and shoot baskets with a basketball when they are upset about something. As their brain changes the way it thinks about the problem, they will become more adept at their movements.

Once their movements are adept, they will have worked through the issue and can move toward a more effective behaviour.

Study kit

Depending on the subject your child is studying, there are ways to allow for deeper learning with the brain by engaging different ways of learning. If your child is working on a math problem, they might approach the problem in these different learning methods.

Auditory

Start by having them read the math problem out loud to themselves and make it into a story. This will help them create a story they can return to that will allow them to understand the problem in way that is useful to them.

They can create as complicated or as simple a story as they like. By repeating the story over and over, they will begin to finish the story by creating an answer or a way of approaching the problem within the story.

Kinesthetic

When the child is working with a math problem, they might want to move their body in the way that makes the problem more sensible to them. For example, if there is a problem with addition, they might want to take items that add up to the different parts of the issue.

This will help them as they move the items from one part of the problem into the solution. They can also begin to count the items as they touch the items allowing them to come to the answer with their touching sensation, rather than just with the numbers on the page.

Visual

A child who is having troubles with a math issue might also want to visualize what is happening in the problem. They can create a story and visualise it in their minds.

This process is easiest to see when working with history facts they need to remember. By taking the time they need to think about what the historical event would have looked like in their mind, they will keep their brain focused on the facts in a way that is helpful to them.

A learning tool kit should include:
- Ways to engage the sense that are strongest for the child
- Different ways of looking at a problem or a solution
- Different resources that will engage different senses

The more your child can develop a new learning process, the easier it will be to apply this toolkit to issues when they come up. This toolkit can be helpful for studying as well as for learning new material.

Here are some hints for creating a teaching and studying kit:
- Have your child ask a lot of questions
- Get your child to determine the reason why the information is important to learn
- Encourage your child to talk about their learning process

As you can see, this allows learning to be more dynamic and more engaging at all levels of their brain's processes. An even more effective way to encourage learning in your child is to have them try to teach what they have learned to you in the way that makes sense to them.

They will need to focus on the learning tools that make sense to them – i.e. metaphors, stories, pictures, etc. From there, they can begin to see where they might need to fill in gaps.

A learning strategy can be broken down into four different parts:
- What does the child need to do?
- What steps can a child take?
- What is the way the child learns?
- How can a child improve their learning (resources, exercises etc.)?

When you break down the learning process in this way, the child will be able to develop their own learning process for each subject in a proactive and effective way. They will also have the satisfaction of learning in a way that makes sense to them.

Should a teacher begin to tell them they should learn in another way, they can then go back and review the steps they need to take that will make sense to them.

All of the teaching styles can be adjusted through reframing and through breaking up the information in a positive way.

Creative trio

Creative people have creative ways of looking at the things they want to create and the issues that might come up as a result. By creating more than one "eye" to look at the task at hand, the child can see the different ways in which they can approach their next step in the task.

The three "eyes" that might be helpful for your child include:
- The Dreamer
- The Realist
- The Critic

These three eyes allow for different ways of looking the project. For example, your child might be wondering how to develop their school plans and goals for their future.

The Dreamer is the eye that thinks anything is possible. From this perspective, a child might create a terrific plan that includes the possibility that they can do everything they want to do when they want to do it.

Let's say your child wants to be an astronaut. Before he begins, have him access an anchor that makes him feel powerful and happy and hopeful.

Once he is in this state of mind, the work can begin. From the Dreamer perspective, the sky is the limit, no pun intended. Your kid might think of all of the things he can do when he is an astronaut. This might include flying to the moon, to other planets and beyond.

This is the fun phase in which he will be able to say anything and believe anything is possible. He might begin to show this part of the conversation as:
- A story of his success
- A picture of an astronaut
- Trying on a space suit

A child will love this part of the process—that is certain. Even adults love this part of the creative process. By anchoring into the feeling that anything is possible, this also becomes an anchor for their dream.

Next, the child will want to anchor into the idea of the Realist. When he is in this state, he might think about the things he needs to do in order to get into an astronaut program.
- Go to school
- Attend astronaut training programs
- Become physically fit

Thinking of a time when he took steps that lead to success, have your child think about how it feels to be successful in the steps that lead to certain outcomes.

Once he has anchored that idea, have him think about being an astronaut again. He will think about those positive feelings and he will feel confident in relation to the steps he wants to take.

Finally, the Critic is the perspective that examines all the possible issues that might crop up. Have your child think about a time when he had to approach someone who was not in agreement with something he did. Get him to remember a time when he was able to argue effectively or he was able to ignore the criticisms of someone else.

This feeling should then be anchored along with the idea of being an astronaut.

Finally, with all of these ideas in mind, let him choose three different chairs in a room and assign each one to the "eye" that is seeing the problem—or the idea of being an astronaut.

In the Dreamer chair, he should sit down and ask himself these questions:
- What will I get to do?
- What are the benefits?
- What is the future for this career?
- What will I achieve?
- What is the purpose?
- How will I know when I've succeeded?
- What kind of person will I become?

In the Realist chair, they should sit and ask:
- What do I need to do?
- How will I do what needs to be done?
- Where will I do what needs to be done?
- How can I measure my progress?
- What do I need to reach my goal?

In the Critic chair, they should sit and ask:
- How will my life change?
- How will others in my life be affected?
- What are the benefits of not becoming an astronaut?
- What might be an obstacle to success?
- What should I avoid?
- What is the best timing?

The child can then have these answers in their mind and move back to the Dreamer chair. In that chair, the child can then begin to come up with solutions to any problems the Critic might have brought up.

In the Realist chair, the child can go back to figure out what things may not have been supported by the Critic.

This process continues until all of the different questions have been answered and all of the "eyes" of the chairs have been able to agree on what the child needs to do.

Swishing beliefs

If there is a limiting belief your child has and you want to stop, the swishing method is a good way to use NLP to adjust the way your child thinks. What you need to do is to create a swish pattern with the child's brain, which will allow those limiting beliefs to be moved out of their consciousness.

Here's what you will need to do with your child:
- Think about something that is unsure in the child's life.
- Think about a strong conviction—something the child believes strongly.

Make sure to use all of the different types of senses to ensure this belief is solid in the child's mind:
- Consider a limiting belief. What does your child think might limit them in their lives?

- Think of a replacement belief. What could a child begin to believe that would dissolve the limiting belief?
- Tell your child to close their eyes and picture their limiting belief in any way they want. Have them anchor this picture and to visualise this belief as strongly as they can
- Once they have the picture in their head, have them picture the belief blowing up or rocketing off into space
- Tell your child to picture the positive replacement belief in their mind. Have them anchor into this picture and picture this belief as strongly as they can
- Once they have the picture firmly in their head, have them picture this positive belief rocketing off into space as well
- Continue to do this process six or seven times until the positive and the replacement beliefs are out of the child's conscious mind

Make sure the rocketing process only takes a few seconds. This is where the "swish" comes in. These ideas should move away from the child's mind as quickly as possible, in less time than it takes to say "swish".When this happens, the child will be able to let go of any limiting beliefs they might have. At the same time they will replace them with positive beliefs, deep in their mind.This is quick, easy to do, and works on adults too.

Clarity builders

If you want to make sure your child is able to look at all the different ideas during a class or during a family meeting, you might want to teach them to try on different hats.

These hats can be named anything you like, so long as you define them clearly for everyone in the family or in the group—or just for your child.

When the child puts on these different hats, they will look at the information or the problem in a new way. Here are some of the hats they might want to wear:[40]

- **White hat:** This is the hat that might look at the facts or the data that is surrounding a question or an issue. This will help to start a conversation that involves a child or it can be the beginning of a school concern. What are the facts?
- **Black hat:** Also known as the devil's advocate, this is the hat that looks at what might go wrong or what could be safety issues about a situation or a question
- **Red hat:** This hat discusses what a person feels about a situation, regardless of the facts. What does the child feel right now in his or her gut?
- **Yellow hat:** When wearing this hat, the person will take on the most positive outlook they can. What are the positive feelings or concerns that come up surrounding the question or concern?
- **Blue hat:** What is the process that a person can take in terms of the question or the problem? This hat is put on when action steps need to be created. Overview or big picture thinking
- **Green hat:** When a child wears the green hat, they are encouraged to be creative. The more creative, the better. There are no limitations when a person wears this hat

As you can see, there are a lot of hats a child can wear when they are thinking about a problem. They might want to create actual hats to help them remember what questions they need to ask or you might want to create different coloured cards to put out that will help remember what hat everyone is wearing.

These hats are particularly effective during a family meeting. Since everyone is wearing the same hat at the same time, all will be able to say what they need to say, and no one feels left out of the discussion.

Discarding old beliefs

Your child, and you, will benefit greatly from discarding old beliefs in the midst of learning how to learn more effectively. After all, all of those old beliefs can get in the way of new and exciting beliefs.

There is a belief cycle that you may want to acknowledge, as it is something that all of us experience:
- You have a belief
- You learn about the belief and you believe in it even more strongly
- You begin to learn opposing information
- You begin to doubt the belief
- You begin to open to the possibility of believing something different
- You research a new belief
- You gather facts and arguments for the new belief
- You create a new belief

This cycle can continue again and again—and it does during your lifetime. Beliefs change because we change. When a belief isn't serving us anymore, it may be a good idea to look for ways to change the belief or to open up to the possibility of new beliefs.

One of the ways you and your child can begin to let go of old beliefs is to visit the Museum of Old Beliefs.

Designed by author and NLP trainer Robert Dilts, this exercise can help to break old belief patterns and ideas. After this exercise, you can then use the swish pattern of changing beliefs to help your child begin to be able to change the way their brain works and the beliefs it holds:
1) Write out six different phrases on six different pieces of paper:
2) Current belief
3) Open to doubt

4) Museum of Old Beliefs
5) Absolutely true
6) Open to believing
7) New belief
8) Put all of these pieces on the floor, with the top three listed papers in a row of three
9) Place the second three pieces of paper on the floor below the top three, leaving about one to two feet of space between the papers so it's easy to move from one to the other
10) Start by having your child stand at "Open to Doubt"
11) Have them think about a belief that isn't working for them and think about what it would mean to be open to doubting that it's true
12) Have the child go to another part of the room to let this feeling go
13) Have the child go to "Museum of Old Beliefs"
14) Have the child think about the other beliefs they used to have that they no longer believe to be true. This might include everything from the Tooth Fairy to Santa Claus.
15) Have them think about how they feel about these beliefs no longer being true for them
16) Have the child go to another part of the room to let this feeling go
17) Have the child go to "Open to Believing"
18) Have the child think about something they don't quite believe, but they are considering believing in the future.
19) Have them stand here and think about what it would be like to believe this new belief
20) Have the child go to another part of the room to let this feeling go
21) Have the child go to "Absolutely True"
22) Have the child think about things they believe to be absolutely true. Have them think about several different situations that are absolutely true for them
23) Have the child go to another part of the room to let this feeling go
24) Have the child do to "Current Belief".
25) Have the child think about a belief that might be limiting

them in some way. Have them think about this belief and what it means to them right now

26) Have the child step to "Open to Doubt". There, have them think about what it might mean to be open to doubt about this limiting belief

27) Have them move to "Museum of Old Beliefs" and think about the limiting belief as something that could become an old belief, something they used to believe in

28) Have the child stand at "New Belief"

29) In that position, have the child think about what their new belief will be to replace the limiting one

30) From there, have the child step to "Open to Believing"

31) In that position, have your child think about the possibility of being able to believe in this new belief

32) Have the child step onto "Absolutely True"

33) Have the child stop and think about what it means to believe this new belief is absolutely true

With the new belief, have the child repeat the last few steps again and again until they begin to internalise the new belief and it replaces their old belief.

This is a lengthy exercise, so make sure to leave plenty of time to complete it.

Journaling

While journaling isn't something that is merely for NLP, it can provide an ideal way to document the various processes the child is using when they are working with their brain.

They might want to create a list of goals they want to achieve with NLP or they might want to create notes after they do certain NLP exercises.

Encourage your child to create a journal that will help them to track the way they are creating their own beliefs, but then empower them to use the exercises (with your help) when they want to make changes. It's a powerful combination and can lead to greater retention of information. As always, there appears to be another side to the memory "coin".

Our memory is a strange beast as Gestalt psychologist Bluma Zeigarnik noticed a funny thing: waiters in a Vienna restaurant could only remember orders that were in progress.[41] As soon as the order was sent out and complete, they seemed to wipe it from memory.

Zeigarnik then did what any good psychologist would: she went back to the lab and designed a study. A group of adults and children were given anywhere between 18 and 22 tasks to perform (both physical ones, like making clay figures, and mental ones, like solving puzzles). Only, half of those tasks were interrupted so they couldn't be completed. At the end, the subjects remembered the interrupted tasks far better than the completed ones, over two times better, in fact.

Zeigarnik ascribed the finding to a state of tension, akin to a cliffhanger ending: Your mind wants to know what comes next. It wants to finish. It wants to keep working—and it will keep working even if you tell it to stop. All through those other tasks, it will subconsciously be remembering the ones it never got to complete.

Socrates' reproach in The Phaedrus that the written word is the enemy of memory appears to hold some truth. He seems to be describing the Zeigarnik effect centuries before her research. In the dialogue, Socrates recounts the story of the god Theuth, or Ammon, who offers the king Thamus the gift of letters:
"This," said Theuth, "will make the Egyptians wiser and give them better memories; it is a specific both for the memory and for the wit."
Thamus replied, "O most ingenious Theuth, the parent or inventor of an art is not always the best judge of the utility or inutility of his own inventions to the users of them.
"And in this instance, you who are the father of letters, from a

paternal love of your own children have been led to attribute to them a quality which they cannot have; for this discovery of yours will create forgetfulness in the learners' souls, because they will not use their memories; they will trust to the external written characters and not remember of themselves."

"The specific which you have discovered is an aid not to memory, but to reminiscence, and you give your disciples not truth, but only the semblance of truth; they will be hearers of many things and will have learned nothing; they will appear to be omniscient and will generally know nothing; they will be tiresome company, having the show of wisdom without the reality."

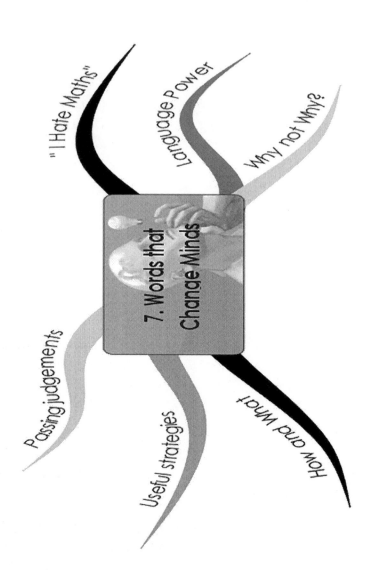

Chapter 7
Words That Change Minds

"I keep six honest serving-men,
(They taught me all I knew);
Their names are What and Why and When
And How and Where and Who.
I send them over land and sea,
I send them east and west;
But after they have worked for me,
I give them all a rest."

Rudyard Kipling
(Excerpt from The Elephant's Child)

"I Hate Math, I Hate Teachers and I Hate School"

John's presenting problem, as stated above, was keeping him from having fun and enjoying learning. He had taken a small piece of information and blown it out of proportion. This is a process we as therapists/coaches call 'chunking'.

John then generalises his thoughts through time and space with his hatred of math, teachers and school. Matt's challenge was to enable him to bring his thoughts into perspective, or chunk them down. Matt can take it from here.

John believed his hatred to be genuine. I had to meet him in his own world and encourage him to step into a new reality, which would enable him to develop a greater behavioural repertoire.

"Can you love your mother and father?" I asked.
"Yes," came his reply with a kind of "why don't you ask me a

question that I can say no to, because I like saying no", sort of
way.
"Can you enjoy spending time with them?"
"Yes," the reply came again, but this time with a sort of, "the
answers from here must all be yes," look upon his face
"And has your mother and father ever shown you how to do
stuff?
"Yes," another positive response.
The idea was to build, what is known in hypnosis, as "the yes
set" where the practitioner uses "truisms", which are irrefutable
statements of truth or fact.

For example, if I had said: "Do you love your mother and
father?" John has the opportunity to say no, as right at that
moment he might be feeling differently towards them. Yet, by
asking, "Can you love your mother and father?" I have created
a truism because it is possible that John can love his mother
and father at some point in time. Three of these truisms in
succession use Newton's Law of Inertia: When you begin to
nod your head and think "yes", then you will continue to do this
until some other, external force impacts upon you.

Now, John was nodding away, and I began to connect, or map
across, his truisms to the things that he hated. It went like this:
"John, are there times when you sometimes don't like your
mother and father even though you love them, like when you
have to go to bed early or tidy your room or something?" John
nods
"And when you are snuggled comfortably in your warm bed
and your room is tidy and that feels good, can you accept that
you are learning how to feel good at the same time that your
parents are teaching you stuff without you even noticing that
you are being taught?"
John nods again
"So, your parents are actually really good teachers, are they
not?"
At the end of the sentence I used a "tag question" which
compounds the "yes set" even further because every time you
hear a tag question you find yourself agreeing. You do, don't

you? You're getting the hang of this, aren't you? John smiled and acknowledged that, yes indeed, his parents are good teachers, so his model of the world is beginning to expand. "Really, so when you think about it, there are learnings in everything that you do, aren't there," I prodded him some more?

"I suppose so," John conceded.

"So, if a place that you learn is a school, then does that mean that your house is a school too?"

John smiled acceptingly.

"Hmmm! I wonder if you would like one sweet or two sweets or maybe even three or more."

"More!" John barked. I offered John one sweet and he pointed out that I had mentioned "more".

"Oh?" I wondered, "You are able to understand that math helps you to get more goodies, are you?"

"Yeah, yeah, yeah, yeah, yeah!" He exclaimed in a sort of Scooby Doo kind of way.

Mum and dad reported back that John was now enjoying school even though they couldn't figure out what it was that I had done, after all it just seemed like a conversation, much like the many they had had over the preceding year. Yet, now John has changed.[42]

The Power of Language

After the preceding chapters you have probably noticed just how valuable words can be. The development of language is thought to happen through talking and listening to those around us. There is some disagreement, however, about how the rules of syntax are gained. Here again there are two main schools of thought:

1. **Nature** – by which some principles are innate and are transmitted through the human genome.
2. **Nurture** – where learning the rules come wholly from linguistic input.

The "nature" position, championed by linguist and cognitive scientist Noam Chomsky, argues that language is a unique human accomplishment.[37] His claim is based upon the view that what children hear—their linguistic input—is not sufficient to explain how they come to learn language. So they must possess an innate LAD (Language Acquisition Device). This claim has been prevalent for over fifty years and remains influential.

The "nurture" position claimed by, amongst others, Elizabeth Bates, a professor in psychology and cognitive science, suggests there is enough information in the linguistic input that children receive, and therefore there is no need to assume an innate language acquisition device.[38] Bates was well known for her assertion that linguistic knowledge is distributed throughout the brain.

Why?

You've heard this question and you will continue to hear this question as soon as children learn the word. Though this is a word that will certainly open up new doors and new possibilities for your child, there is a way to use the question to encourage an even deeper level of learning for them.

Why should you answer why? Let's find out.
The story of why begins with a child's experience of the world. Kids see all of these things going on around them and they have no idea what's happening or why things are happening.

All they know how to do is to gather information. They want to know more and more and more since their brain is able to handle that.

The question why will begin to create more and more questions that will then begin to form an even larger understanding of the world, for your child. And, at times, your child might even begin to understand that there are endless questions. Or they will at least feel they need to ask just one more...

During this time, it's best that as a parent you answer the question as simply as possible. Remember Albert Einstein said: "If you can't explain it simply, you don't understand it well enough".

Children want to know the answer, but giving them just one answer can lead them to an impoverished map of the world. Like in the following example.

Aiden: "Where does wood come from?"
Dad: "Trees".
This one-word answer is essentially a full stop, and puts an end to the dialogue.
A learning opportunity has presented itself, so why not make the most of it.
Aiden: "Where does wood come from?"
Dad: "Where do you think it comes from?"
Aiden: "We got some from the DIY shop last week".
Dad: "Is there anywhere else wood can come from?"
Aiden: "Well...? You cut the branches off the tree and set a fire, so wood must come from the ground?"
Dad: "Wow, that's interesting! Anywhere else...?"
And on and on you can go, creating more and more synaptic connections.
Goody!
Another thing to keep in mind at this stage is that the child is interpreting and judging their world by what affects them.

So, they ask why:
- Why is the sky blue?
- Why do dogs have fur?
- Why is my juice purple?

The adult brain wants to answer these questions by giving the reasons your child seems to be asking.

The sky is blue because light reflects in the atmosphere, creating a blue colour in the sky. When there is less light, there is a grey sky and when there's no light, like at night, the sky is black.

But this isn't necessarily the explanation children want. What they may need is for you to give them more facts. Instead of talking about why the sky is blue, you could tell them that the sky can also be other colors. You could talk about how the sky changes when there are storms and when it's nighttime.

Yes, you're not actually answering their question, but you're probably giving your child more information. That's what they want. They want to know more and that's why they ask why.

Of course, a child might also want to get your attention and asking "why?" is certainly going to do that. If you answer their question quickly, they are bound to ask you "why?" again. And again. And again.

The more you answer, the more time they are getting with their parent, which is going to make them very happy. It's up to you to continue to answer their whys, but do keep these ideas in mind:

- Answering is a tangent
- It gives new ideas
- Don't limit the answer
- Focus on facts, as well as reasoning
- Sometimes respond to a why with: "What do you think?"
- If you don't know the answer, let them see you write down the question and "research" the answer together at the library or at the museum. In this way you can have fun together and the child knows that you take questions seriously

The "why", you as an adult, might ask of another person is designed to find out how things work. But the "why" your child is asking of you is designed to add more information to their brain.

This is something that makes all the difference when you speak to them.

The challenges of why

Think about the last time that someone challenged you by asking "why?" When you were sharing a story or you were talking about a new idea, as soon as you heard "why?" from the other person, you might have simply responded with, "Because".

Sometimes you just don't want to defend what you think. You just want to tell the story and move on. Children are the same way. The challenges of "why" include:

Resistance to learning

When the idea of "why" is echoed back to a child, they don't know how to answer it. Or they answer in a way that doesn't make sense to you. In either case, they begin to think that "why" is something that prevents them from learning in the way they want to learn.

After all, for children, "why" doesn't actually ask "why?" All it's asking is for more information

Possible bad information

If you don't know the answer, then you might begin to give your child information that is incorrect. Yes, they can learn the right facts later, but why do this to a kid?

Unending questioning

When you aren't answering the "why" question, or you're not answering it to the child's satisfaction, it's going to turn into unending questions

Parents too are challenged by the idea of "why" since it can bring up issues for them too. After all, you don't necessarily know the answer to every question that your child asks you, do you? Probably not. All you know is that your child is asking you question after question... and you're just getting tired of answering. So you begin to make up information.

While your child might not catch onto this for a bit, once they do, they will begin to question everything they are taught. This isn't entirely bad, but it can halt the learning process. A child who doesn't think the lessons they are learning are true, is a child who may have troubles in school and who might have troubles at home. But if you switch to the idea of what something is instead of why, you can focus on learning things together.

You can go to the library, museum or the internet and find out what something is and then you can both retain that knowledge. Or you can learn about the "why" of a particular topic when you begin to research the answer to "what".

Not why

Does a child always have to ask "why"? That's a question many parents, caregivers and teachers have wanted to have answered. They have also wanted to know whether there are other questions that might be more effective. How are you feeling now? In our experience 'why' questions can be unhelpful to say the least. There is little researched evidence to support our claim other than experience. So what to do if your child asks that question nevertheless?

Introducing how and what

There are two responses to your kids' questioning that will help them learn much more effectively: "what?" and "how?" When you respond this way, your child begins to ask these questions themselves, and as a result they will begin to see that there is more information available in asking different questions. And they will want to keep that up.

They will begin to see that when they ask what something is, they get a bunch of cool facts. Children find that when they ask "how?" something works, they learn a story about how things fit together.

Children want to have the stories and the colour details that they envision in their heads. They want to have more experiences in their everyday lives. They want to learn.

By encouraging them to learn in a way that supports the way their brains are working, you allow them to continue to want to learn. And from there, the possibilities are endless. You can introduce the idea of "what" and "how" in a number of ways:

Reframe the question

It might be easiest to simply reframe the question with the words "what" and "how". This can encourage your child to begin to mimic this question in order to get certain answers.

Ask the question yourself

You might also want to repeat their question, but say it as though you're asking it as well. This then becomes a team effort to answer the question the child is asking.

Let's find out…

When you begin to create the team effort, talk about how the both of you can find out how something works or what the object is.

Create a positive experience when the child is learning and it all begins with asking the best questions. "Why" isn't a bad question. There are just better questions to ask. All your child knows is that they have certain pieces of information in their mind and they want to know more. They don't necessarily want to actually know why, but they do want to know what else there is to know.

What else?

When the question of "why?" is used when teaching or interacting with a child, it can cause them to stop being as excited to learn what else there is in the world.

Not that they will stop learning, of course, but the question of "why?" can create more of a challenge for them. Remember the threat response from the limbic brain?

Instead, it's a good idea to focus on what:
- What is an apple?
- What is a fruit?
- What is a food?

When you create clear ideas about the question the child has, they will begin to categorise the information they have. They will be able to have a better understanding of what they know and why it's important they know it. For example, if a child asks why they are having dinner, you can turn it around into what they are having for dinner:
- What are we eating? Food
- What kind of food? Spaghetti
- What does spaghetti include? Noodles and meatballs

As you can see, this conversation is not challenging to a child. It's a new way of looking at the facts of what is happening and what is being presented to a child.

By steering the conversation towards "what", you will create a conversation that is satisfying to the child and it will help them to think about what they are experiencing. They will begin to look at the world as things and categories, which will help shape their later learning.

As a child develops, being able to ask them 'what' will also help them to direct their own answers to ideas they easily recognise. When they are answering their questions, they are thinking about the question and the answer, but they aren't speculating about why it is important: They are simply using the facts they know and retelling them.

This is a simpler and more effective learning process for many children. They don't feel they need to defend their answers, only that they need to relate them to another person. And that's going to speed up the learning process.

Communication Strategies to Use

When you're working with your child, it's easy to use communication strategies you've always used. After all, that's what has worked in the past.

But when you want to promote learning and you want to promote growth, you often need to change your own communication style. And this isn't necessarily a negative thing.

This is not to say that your communication is "wrong" or that it needs to be fixed. Rather, look at these suggestions as opportunities to become an even better parent to your child. Communication strategies can help you encourage your child to speak more and to learn more from their environment.

Some of these tips include information you've already learned, while other times they include strategies that work with adults as well.

Using "I" statements

One of the best ways to communicate with anyone is to talk about I rather than you. When you speak from your experience, then you will be able to focus only on what you know. This allows you to create open communication with a child that does not promote defensiveness. If you talk about you and what the child thinks, then you're not letting them speak for themselves, and you might be interpreting their thoughts incorrectly.

Instead of looking to speak for your child, present your own ideas and then you can begin to create a positive conversation. Here's an example of a different way of stating something:

> **You are being unreasonable. I feel affected by the way you're acting.**

Yes, there is still a "you" in there, but you're talking about what you are experiencing instead of accusing the other person of being one way or the other. Focus today on bringing more "I" statements into your conversations you will begin to see that you are more effective in teaching them. And your kids will be more willing to listen.

What's even better about the process of adding more "I" statements into your own conversations is that your child will begin to do the same. They will begin to talk about what they think, without assuming that others think a certain way. Their conversational style becomes productive and balanced, allowing them to learn more along the way.

Focus on...?

When you are speaking with your kids it's important to decide where to place your focus. Adults use strategies other than child-directed speech like recasting, expanding, and labelling to embellish the communication.

Recasting is paraphrasing, perhaps turning it into a question or restating the child's sentence as a fully formed sentence.

Expanding is restating, in a more sophisticated way, what the child said.

Labelling is identifying the names of things.
There will be times when you want to speak about feelings, sharing and labelling your own feelings, to help them understand their own. If you focus on their understanding of the facts of a situation or a lesson, it will allow a child who is trying to learn the opportunity to take in those facts, and to store them until they are ready to be used again.

If you are unable to find facts, then you may need to focus on how you can find out together, modeling research strategies and collecting data, for example:

> **I was affected when I came home and saw that the vase was on the ground. I felt sad that the vase was broken.**

This is simple, non-accusatory and it allows the child to respond in a meaningful manner. When you simply state the facts and how you feel about them, you are able to create a non-judgmental atmosphere. And a child will see that you're responding to the facts,

not to the action (assuming they are the one that dropped the vase).
The more you focus on what has actually happened, the

easier it will be to focus on how to respond, instead of lashing out at the actual event. This moves a difficult situation into a problem that simply needs to be solved. And your child doesn't need to feel bad anywhere in the process.

What they are learning is that actions and events have consequences. And if they don't like the way that something has affected another person, they can make alternative choices in the future.

Be respectful

When you are speaking with your child, should you be anything but respectful? Your child has just as much a right to say something to you and to feel a certain way, as you have a right to do the same.

You will show your child the proper way to treat others when you begin to show respect to them. No matter what happens between you, make sure you are completely respectful of their feelings, their ideas, and their conclusions.

You don't have to agree with them, but you also don't have to tell them that they are wrong. They can believe anything they like. You might challenge their understanding of the facts, but there is no need to "correct" their feelings. Those are your child's to understand and to adjust as necessary.

Be supportive

When your child is talking, they are looking for you to support them. They want to know that anything they say and do is going to be accepted by the people they love the most: their parents.

Whenever your child is speaking or they are talking about their experience, it's a good idea to tell them that you support their ideas. You can admit to not agreeing, but you should support them. Support might come in a number of different ways:

- Saying that you support them
- Helping a child learn more
- Encouraging a child to take action when needed
- Asking more questions to fully understand what they mean

Support isn't just about trying to make sure your child is right. You can support their learning process too. When you do this, it allows a child to feel like they are able to have help whenever they need it. They will know that you are someone to whom they can turn when they need support and assistance.

Support is something that speaks volumes about your connection to your child and about your commitment to their learning. How can you support your child?

A child's voice

"The essence of the demand for freedom is the need of conditions which will enable an individual to make his own special contribution to a group interest, and to partake of its activities in such ways that social guidance shall be a matter of his own mental attitude, and not a mere authoritative dictation of his acts."
John Dewey Author, Democracy and Education

Sometimes, a child who has a new idea might want to talk about this idea again and again, going off into tangents, which might not make a lot of sense to you. While you might understand what they mean, you might not be able to fully appreciate their thought process.

So you might want to interrupt them.
It's tempting, that's for sure, but it's not going to help your child feel supported. When you interrupt something she was going to say, you are telling your child that your ideas, words and thought are more important than her own.

As a result, she might not want to talk to you again about things she has on their mind. Or she may begin to stop finding new things to share with you. You want to make sure your children have the opportunity to speak with you. But what about when you're busy? That's when things can be tricky. Here are some ways that you can begin to make space for them to talk with you so they feel heard:

Let them know you want to talk

Just the fact that you want to talk will mean the world to them. Let them know by looking them in the eye that you do want to talk with them. If you have time right at that moment, talk then.

Create time for talking

It might help for you to have a time every day when you are scheduled to talk with each other. This will help you both to feel like you have time together that will be special and that will build your relationship.

Schedule time if you're busy

If you are busy or you are doing something that might keep you distracted when you talk with them, make an appointment for a later time. Schedule a time to chat that's free from interruptions. And keep the "appointment". Or, create a task that involves you both working and talking together.

Encourage other forms of communication

If you notice that your child has troubles talking to you one-on-one, then you might want to encourage email or notes between each other. This will help you to continue to have a clear method of communication, but it will also help you to become more comfortable with talking.

Listen

Yes, if you're talking with your child, you need to make sure you're listening more than you're talking. Make sure you listen intently and that you show them you are listening by nodding your head or telling them that you understand.

Repeat what you've heard

When your child is finished, make sure to repeat to them the highlights of what they have told you. This will help them realise that you have indeed learned what they have said.

Thank them for speaking,

At the end, it's a good idea to thank your child for speaking to you. Show them that you treasure this time and they will be encouraged to talk more.

When you give your child your undivided attention, this is worth more than many other things you can give them. Plus, a child who feels comfortable talking with you is also going to be more comfortable listening to what you have to share too.

The effects of passing judgments

Sometimes, you might think the ideas they have are wrong. While you might think this, it is important not to express this. Children's' ideas are something to cultivate. They are learning about the world around them and the more they learn, the better they will become at learning. If you pass judgment on what they have learned, they will either stop talking to you or they will stop learning about a certain topic.

And you don't want to limit them in that way. Being critical of the learning process can stifle it and it can cause a child to feel as though they aren't doing something the right way. Instead, offer your own opinion on the subject and then let them know that you value what they have said too. Perhaps combining both of your views creates something more coherent than each thought on its own.

You can both have your own ideas and not agree—a valuable lesson for a learner to take out into the world.

Avoid gossip

In order for your child to feel as though she is being respected, it's a good idea to avoid gossip of any kind. Kids pick up the habits that adults display, after all.
When you gossip, they learn:
- You don't have to respect others
- Confidentiality isn't important
- They should talk about others
- They might be talked about behind their backs too

This isn't a safe feeling for them. Instead, focus on talking only about your experience and about your feelings. If you want to talk about another person, then do so with respect and without breaking any confidentiality rules.

A good rule of thumb is to think about what you might say if that other person was in the room. If you wouldn't say what you want to say when they are in the room, then you probably shouldn't say it at all.

Feeling safe

No matter the conversation, you want to make sure that kids feel safe when they talk to you. This will help them to feel comfortable about talking in general. Plus, they will know they can talk freely and not be judged or criticised.

You can make your kids feel safe by being open, being honest, keeping secrets when needed and not criticising them. When you are honest with your child, she knows you are going to be honest with her all the time.

You don't want to give your child any reason to feel like she might not be hearing the truth from you. True, sometimes, you might not want to tell the truth, but it's something that will show you respect your children and their relationship to you. If they tell you something in confidence, keep it a secret, assuming it's not something that hurts someone.

The more you can encourage open communication with others, the more they will create the same sort of conversations with others. And interacting in the world in this positive way will only promote learning throughout their life.

Creating a Free School

This chapter sits well with the philosophy of A.S. Neill, the founder of Summerhill School, who believed "the function of a child is to live his own life—not the life that his anxious parents think he should live, not a life according to the purpose of an educator who thinks he knows best."

Did you know Summerhill School was the original free school?

The school functions from three core principles: democracy, equality and freedom. Summerhill successfully defend its philosophies against the British government to remain a free school, and it is still thriving today.

'Summerhill School Wins Court Case'

"Defended by the international human rights barrister, Sir Geoffrey Robertson QC, after three days at the Royal Courts of Justice, Summerhill won its right to continue to be based on children's' rights. The Department for Education accepted its demands, expressed in a joint agreement.

"The agreement was voted on by the children from the school in the courtroom. This agreement accepted the right of children at Summerhill to control their own learning, and has been used by Home Educators as part of their legal fights with the government. Summerhill is now the most legally protected school in the country with a unique inspection process that is the first to include the voices of children, preceding the newly announced Office for Standards in Education (OFSTED) plans to take account of students' views.

"Summerhill is the only school that has direct input into its inspections through legally appointed experts. Its children have continued to lobby for all children to have the rights they have, attending and lobbying at the UN Special Session on the Child (2002) and the UNESCO conference of Education Ministers when a student spoke during the closing ceremony."[43]

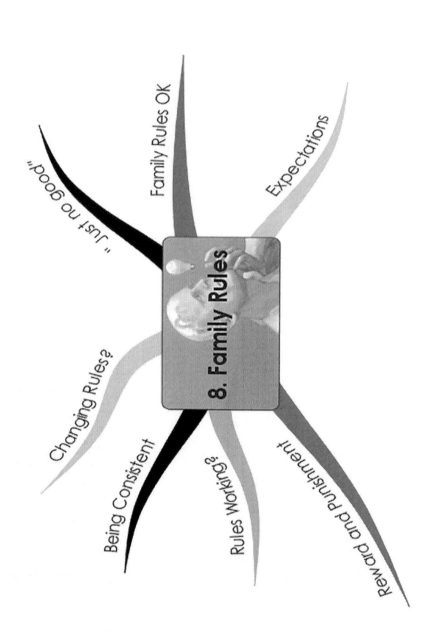

"Just no good"

Family Rules OK

Expectations

Changing Rules?

8. Family Rules

Being Consistent

Rules Working?

Reward and Punishment

Chapter 8
Family Rules

*"If your kid needs a role model and you ain't it, you're both f****d."*
George Carlin, Brain Droppings

"Just No Good at Anything"

Brian was the head of a primary school and he asked me to work with a little lad, we can call Jimmy. Brian explained that the school had tried teaching Jimmy to read, write and do mathematics, which he wasn't engaging in, so they tried various games, sports and activities, again to no avail. Jimmy had no friends and remained isolated, despite the best efforts of his teachers.

The head felt they needed to do more, "Because," Brian said, "I feel terrible for saying this...but...it's like he's just no good at anything."

When I met Jimmy he appeared withdrawn, not shy but not open to connecting. I asked him if there was anything that he enjoyed doing and he replied forlornly, "No, I am just no good at anything." In that instant I could feel both the desperation of his teachers and Jimmy's despair. There was a danger here of me buying into the negativity of the situation and in doing so I would be letting down my young client. I had to create and maintain a highly energetic and positive state of being that would encourage and carry Jimmy along.

"Wow! That's fantastic!" I exclaimed enthusiastically. "How amazing is that?"
Jimmy wasn't used to this type of response to his statement. He just stared with a puzzling look like I was a little crazy,

which is excellent, and just what I was hoping to create. I continued with bags of enthusiasm and asked, "You are always able to not do well at anything?" Jimmy slowly nodded in response. I now had Jimmy primed for a mental shift in his current thinking, because if he is "always able to not do" then he has a below conscious strategy that he can rely on. Therefore, he is exceptionally good at "not doing". "So, who would you be if you were to use this ability, this skill on yourself," I asked, "So that you always failed at stopping yourself from not being good at anything?"

It is important to understand there is a lot going on "behind the scenes" here and for the purpose of making this material accessible I have omitted a lot of information, which practitioners may assume are in place.

Jimmy was now in a "know nothing state", that's when you are just comfortably staring off into space, not consciously thinking about anything in particular, yet your unconscious mind is busy figuring things out and remapping your experiences. Whilst in this state of mind, I brought up a metaphor of an oak tree telling about the oak being king of all of the trees, how big and strong the oak is and how everyone knows about the oak, as it is a very special tree. Jimmy smiled and little by little became more and more engaged… "You're listening," I said in a light enthusiastic way, then I dropped my tone and said, "You are a good listener".

Jimmy gazed at me questioningly and confused. I continued, and matching his curiosity I said: "Did you know that although the oak is huge, strong and well thought of, when he was small and didn't grow quickly, at the same pace as the other trees, people would think he was a little nutty? That's because he needed his own space to grow a little, before feeling good and smiling at others… Imagine that?"
The whole interaction took about an hour and according to Brian, Jimmy had become more open, engaging and had a new group of friends to interact with.

In short his whole outlook had transformed.[44]

Family Rules Okay?

Everybody's experience of the world is impacted by the family dynamics they have and or are growing in. We mentioned earlier that neuroscience supports the view that the brain is designed for survival.

Virginia Satir, the American author and psychotherapist, states that "family rules alone often have enough power to influence our internal reality and even control what we say. Sometimes other significant people or institutions provide our rules.[45] So, parents, caregivers, teachers, peers, religious and cultural role models all can have an effect upon how we develop our family rules.

When they're at home, they are going to interpret and experience their surroundings in a certain way according to the rules of the home, ergo rules from mother to child, father to child, mother and father to child, sibling to sibling, all of these have different rule structures. This Satir believes accounts for many behavioural challenges that arrive outside of the home, because the family rules travel. If this is the case then as Satir points out, "The ingredients of an interaction" explores five factors that influence our pattern of interacting:[46]

1. The family rules we follow for processing information.
2. Our coping style, which reflects our self-worth and gives us the basis for how we hear, feel, react, defend and comment.
3. The way we behave and perceive represents what we learned in the past for our survival.
4. Until we transform the survival patterns that we developed as children we continue to use them.
5. These patterns include how we treat ourselves, how we treat others and how we expect others to treat us.

We gave an example earlier of an employee continuing to use tears when she felt unable to comment on her own behalf. Satir would suggest that this shows the family rule has travelled both in time and context with the person who is now an adult.

This then begs the question: What other rules and patterns of behaviour are running under the surface of you as a parent that you aren't even aware of?

After all, these rules reside in the realms of the unconscious. So, what lessons are you teaching?

The rule structure that you set up for your children's' environment can encourage them to feel safe, content, and they will begin to create positive relationships with those around them—even those outside of the family.

What you need to do is to look into the rules that are present within the learning environment. Rules are important and they can begin to define the way your child can create their lives.

How family rules affect your child

Family rules are often the subject of debate among child psychologists and parents.

Some think that rules are unnecessary, that children should simply run free and make decisions based on the consequences of their actions. Others feel that a strong set of rules will help a child begin to interpret the world in a certain way, while also keeping them safe and protected.

Both arguments have their merit, that's certain, but more important is an awareness of the number of different ways family rules may affect your child.

Rules may:

Help determine right or wrong

When your child walks into the kitchen and throws a plate on the floor, they have broken the rule that you shouldn't throw plates (assuming you have that rule in place). Rules help to set up a basic system of what is right and what is wrong in the family environment

They establish expectations

With rules, children understand the behaviour that's expected of them when they are in certain situations. They begin to appreciate that actions have consequences

They form boundaries

Rules begin to create the sense of boundaries for children, which allows them to understand that there are lines that should not be crossed

They show the need for discipline

When you have rules, you might also have consequences for breaking those rules. A system of punishment might be necessary to ensure that rules are followed

Your child is always learning from the rules you create and the rules you follow. Remember monkey see, monkey do, so step up and show your child that you walk your talk.

Time to upgrade family rules

When you realise that it's time to change the way things are, it's not too late. Sometimes, you might want to give up because you think change is impossible, unrealistic, or simply too difficult.

A better way to look at change, is to look at it as a process that you need to learn. Once you learn what you need to do, you will be able to see changes, to enjoy results, and to appreciate the work you have done.

As you will know by now, NLP (Neuro-Linguistic Programming) is a communication tool that is being effectively used across society. Instead of focusing on the accepted ways to learn, you can begin to create a new system that produces better results—both now and in the future.

Starting today, you can begin to upgrade your family rules by introducing a new program. You're not tossing out what you know, but rather you're bringing in something new. Before you begin, it's a good idea to introduce the realities of your life. Recognising these realities allows you to see just how necessary NLP is in your life now. And how necessary this is for a fulfilling life.

Right and wrong

Rules allow for the concept of right and wrong to develop for a child. When a child is in a situation, they need to know what they can do and what they should not do. While they might not always follow this advice, this is something that can help to inform their decisions.

If the child is out in the world, then they can use these rules to interpret their situations. The child begins to see there are right things to do and wrong things to do, in terms of safety and the well-being of others as well as of themselves.

Virginia Satir would encourage you to transform this black and white, right or wrong approach into a set of guidelines, which in turn, will encourage your child to be flexible and more resilient, when things just happen.[47]

Expectations

We can often carry the assumption that others should know what we expect of them. This is true for any environment—family, school, the workplace and so on. A dialogue concerning everybody involved to clarify what the rule structure is would go a long way in making it clear where everybody stands. Instead of trying to guess what they should do, which can make anyone uncomfortable and unsure of themselves, they will know what they need to do within the environment.

Expectations might include:
- Certain behaviours
- Certain goals
- A certain schedule
- Rules structures
- Family goals

While these expectations might not be clearly defined at first, having a set of expectations in place will allow your child to understand their position both in the family, the organisation and their own life.

Rewards and punishments

When you simply give out punishments, this is not going to cause a child to act in a certain way. True, it will cause them to avoid that behaviour, much of the time. But as there is no alternative, they might actually return to that behaviour.

They might begin to think that since they are getting attention for the bad behaviour, they should continue to do it. After all attention is attention, is it not?

Instead, a system of rewards for good behaviour is a more positive way to encourage family rules to be followed. For example, when you are happy with the behaviour then reward it. And reward it immediately. When you instantly reward a behaviour that is positive, the child will remember what they have done—and they will want to do it more often. The more energy you put toward rewarding and noticing good behaviour, the more they will want to do it.

However, there may be times when your child exhibits a behaviour that is inappropriate. The initial thought might be how do I punish the child? A more constructive thought might be, "What has motivated the child to exhibit that behaviour?" This moment can be a learning experience since you will focus not on the child being "bad", but rather on what are the motivations or drivers behind the behaviour that need to be met—and how?

What are your family rules?

If you think about it right now, what are your family rules? Do you have any? Do you think you need some? Much of the time, we get the family rules we use in our own families from the rules that we followed when we were growing up. And we might not even be aware of that. We simply follow the rules because we have always followed.

But if you want to raise an amazing child, it makes sense to begin to think about what you are teaching your child right now. You want to be more conscious of the rules you teach, and why you want them to be learned and followed.

Remember your covert family rules will be in your blind spot, and you may be acting in ways without you being aware of how you are acting, or why.

Naming your family rules

It's a good idea to sit down with your partner to discuss what rules you have in place right now. And it might even be a good idea to ask the rest of your family which rules they think need to be followed. This can be a very eye-opening experience.

You will want to find out what rules there are, why you chose to include them and whether you think they are working to support the family as a whole.

You might want to write out the rules that your family follows and then post them somewhere that you can look at them often, like on the fridge. Of course, if you're thinking about changing the rules, then you might want to keep this list on a smaller piece of paper.

If you're having troubles thinking of the rules that your family follows, it's a good idea to think about what precedes punishments. In other words, what rules result in punishment when they aren't followed? That will help you begin to see what the patterns are in the rule making and rule breaking.

Take some time when you complete this task since there are bound to be more than just a few rules you have.

Where did your rules come from?

There are a number of places where your rules may have come from. These include your parents, other caregivers, and significant others like friends and siblings. Films and idols can even play a role.

But while these are all valuable sources, you may want to

keep in mind that your family is not like any other family, so you might not want to follow just any other family's rules.

After you think about where your rules came from, you may want to think about where you want your rules to lead. And where you want you to be or what you want to achieve through the family following these rules.

You should have reasons for creating rules in the first place. Be prepared to discuss what the purpose of the rule is.

Are your rules working?

While rules are only a part of what makes the group function, they are a foundation upon which other behaviours can be built and sculpted.

It is a good idea to stop and think about what the rules in your family and what effect they are having. If the rules aren't helping the family to feel supported, then it's time to make a change.

Some points to ponder are:
- Are rules being followed?
- Are there are a lot of punishments?
- Is there a lot of good behaviour?
- How do you feel about the family dynamics?

If family members are having behaviour problems in the home and at school, you might not be creating a strong enough system for them to follow.

A good idea is to think about any issues that might have been coming up in the family, and then to think about whether these were instances of rule breaking or not.

If they were, perhaps it's not that the child is "bad", but that the rules are bad. It never hurts to shake up the rules from time to time anyway, since your goals might be changing, depending on the family dynamics.

As your family matures, you might need to adjust things like performance, feedback and the likes. As times change, so do rules.

Create safety

You can't cross the street when there's a red light because cars will hit you. This is a pretty basic rule, but it illustrates how rules are able to create safety in the world. When you create certain rules at home, family members can begin to feel they will be safe as long as they adhere to certain rules.

Safety comes in a variety of forms: physical, mental and emotional. When you create rules, everyone needs to follow them. This being the case, family members know that everyone is safe and that everyone will continue to be safe— because the rules are in place. Without rules, there is no structure.

Create consistency

When you have a set of rules in a household it also allows you to have a certain idea of consistency. Everyone has to behave in a certain way—or something will happen. Since the child knows this, they know each day what they can expect in their experience if they act in a certain way. This allows them to make choices based on the consequences. It also allows them to not be surprised when something happens in the family.

Of course, consistency can only be achieved if everyone— including the parents follow the same set of rules. And everyone needs to make sure they enforce the rules in a certain way.

Once the rules are not followed as they are supposed to be, a person will begin to doubt their actions and what they need to do next. Remember: "Do as I say not as I do". If parents and caregivers apply this rule of expecting children to listen to their words not duplicate their actions, they create a hypocrisy and many unproductive behaviours will ensue. So, make sure you and significant others are walking the talk.

That's where children can become frustrated and they might begin to act out. They begin to test their environment since they don't know what is expected of them. Rules can create stability and consistency; however, they can also create conflict within contexts, as explained earlier.[48]

Signs You Need to Change the Rules

Not sure if it is time to change the rules within your household? Here are a couple of pointers to help you out, when these are true for your family, it might be time to revisit the rules you created:
- The rules aren't being followed
- There is more negative behaviour
- The rules are worded negatively
- You or your children aren't happy

Every now and again, it's essential to explore your family rules to see if they are working, and behaviour is always a good indicator whether rules are working in harmony or not. Therefore disharmony could be interpreted as a dysfunctional rule structure.

Should children help develop rules?

In some families, it becomes apparent that the rules are not working out. While this might be obvious, how to fix them is not always as clear. Children should be a part of the rule making process. Since the rules are for the entire family, everyone should be involved. This will create a sense of unity and it will help your family begin to work as a team. Whenever

a child or anyone suggests a rule, ask them these questions:
- Is this fair?
- What are the consequences of not following the rule?
- Why is the rule in place?
- How can the rule be followed by everyone?
- What do we do if the rule isn't working?

When you begin to ask what might happen if the rule is in place, you will be able to see any troubles that might crop up before they do. Of course, rules that protect the health and the well-being of others in the family are not disputable. But children can often bring up good points that need to be considered. And it involves them in the creation of a happy family.

A system of punishment

Punishment has been shown to be consistently ineffective as a means of changing behaviour. First, any behavioural changes that comes about as the result of punishment, usually doesn't last very long. As Psychologist and Behaviourist B.F. Skinner explains in his book, About Behaviourism, "Punished behaviour is likely to reappear after the punitive consequences are withdrawn."[49]

Possibly the most important lesson to note is the fact that punishment does not actually offer any new information about more appropriate future behaviours. While kids may be learning to not perform certain actions, they are not really learning anything about what they should be doing.

It has been suggested that occasional spanking is not detrimental, especially when used alongside other forms of discipline. But, in a thorough meta-analysis of earlier research, psychologist Elizabeth Gershoff found that spanking was associated with poor parent-child relationships as well as with increases in antisocial behaviour, delinquency and aggressiveness.[50]

Time-out

Similarly with the nature-nurture debate, psychologists are divided over the "time-out" strategy. The online parenting resource, Ask Dr. Sears, proposes the following top ten tips for an effective time-out:

1. **Give lots of "time-in"**: Positive reinforcement means giving the child lots of positive "time-in" with a connected style of parenting. Then if the child misbehaves, this positive parental input is briefly withdrawn.
2. **Prepare the child:** Help your child connect their behaviour with the time-out. Time-out in your arms or sitting next to you is preferable if the toddler finds the chair too threatening; but you run the risk he'll discover the way to get picked up and held is to misbehave. You can avoid this by holding your child a lot when he is behaving well – which leads us back to the concept of time-in.
3. **Keep time-out brief**: Escort your toddler to the time-out place immediately after the misbehaviour.
4. A prompt, cool, matter-of-fact approach aborts many protests. Keep the time brief – **around one minute per year of age.**
5. **Keep time-out quiet:** This is not the time for your child to be screaming, or for you to be preaching or moralising. If there's a lesson you want your child to hear, save it for later when she'll be open to it.
6. **You be the timer**: An egg timer or alarm clock makes a more lasting impression and helps you keep track of the time.
7. **Pick the right place**: You may have a designated time-out chair or stool for the child. To make the point, the retreat needs to be a boring place. The TV is not on for time-out!
8. **What if your child refuses to go or stay in time-out**: Sit with them, and if necessary keep putting them back physically and give them the message, "I'm the adult here. We are taking time-out."

9. **Time-out for thought**: Time-out gives your older child a chance to reflect on their deeds, and it also gives you a chance to cool off and plan a strategy. This is not a time for preaching or haranguing, rather matter-of-factly tell your child how you expect her to spend the time-out period. The most lasting impression is made when the child realises the consequences of her actions on her own. That's self-discipline.

10. **Clear the air**: After the time-out is over, it's over. The child has served his time and it's time to get on with the day. Convey to him that you now expect him to play nicely and quietly. Possibly orchestrate a new activity.

11. **Parents as referees**: If you get a sense that your kids are getting over-stimulated and things are out of control. Call a halt to the action, remove a few of the toys, separate the children, or change activities.

According to Dr. Sears, "not only does time-out help children behave, it also helps parents. Time-out stops misbehaviour and gives you time to plan your next move."[51] Supporters of time-out claim that is not a form of punishment. Using words like "consequence", "renewal time", or "down time" to make the strategy appear friendly. However, this language may have misled parents into thinking the approach is harmless.

Time-out is seen as a punishment from the child's perspective. It means being isolated from the family and totally disregarded. This is likely to be viewed by children as abandonment and loss of love, which we simply do not agree with.

Parents have been led to believe that children will use time-out to think about what they did and regain some self-control. Actually, when children act in inappropriate, aggressive, or intolerable ways, they are often concealing strong pent-up feelings. It will be almost impossible for them to think rationally. Now is your chance to be an attentive listener who encourages the honest expression of their feelings. This will allow your child to experience new learning and support you both in developing stronger bonds and different behaviours.

Embracing children who lash out physically can be more beneficial than isolating them. It is paradoxical, yet true: "children are most in need of loving attention when they act least deserving of it."[52] Asking anyone who is agitated to sit quietly rarely accomplishes anything other than a backlash.

Rewards and penalties to use

When you want to reward good behaviour (and you should), it's a good idea to have a number of rewards in place that will encourage even more of these good actions. Children who want to be a part of the action will respond well to the idea of a time-in. Younger children, especially, want to feel like they are a part of something fun. As children get older, they might want to have other rewards:

Sticker chart

Whenever a child does something good, you might want to put a sticker on a chart that a younger child can see. They will want to earn more stickers, so they'll continue to act positively.

Tokens

When a child is older, they might want physical rewards for good behaviour. Whenever they do something right or they have a positive day, they earn a token, which can then be saved up for prizes and things they want.

Praise

Every child wants and deserves praise for following the rules and for doing good things. Make sure the praise is rich feedback relative to the task in hand. Avoid simple statements like "well done", which might leave the child uncertain of what was done well. Be specific, and remember to praise their effort.

According to Carol Dweck, it has become a common practice

to praise students for their performance on easy tasks, to tell them they are smart when they do something quickly and perfectly. "When we do this we are not teaching them to welcome challenge and learn from errors. We are teaching them that easy success means they are intelligent and, by implication, that errors and effort means they are not". What should we do if students have had an easy success and come to us expecting praise? "We can apologise for wasting their time and direct them to something more challenging. In this way we may teach them that a meaningful success requires effort. Praising students' intelligence gives them short bursts of pride, followed by a long string of negative consequences," she continues.[53]

Rules about Rules

Yes, there are rules that you should follow when it comes to creating rules in the family. Here are some of the guidelines we recommend:

- Everyone can be involved
- Talk about how everyone should feel in the family
- Share problems with behaviour
- Share ideas for rules
- Keep rules simple
- Keep rules specific
- Decide on rewards
- Decide on penalties/time-out
- Limit the family rules
- Change rules as needed

And remember, rules are in place to help everyone.

Do teachers know best?

This was a rule we had as children along with "adults know best" and any other "rule" about questioning authority. Is it possible for the authority to get it wrong? See if you can answer the following as **true or false**:

1. Your brain is set and unchanging before you even get to school.
2. Kids only use a small percentage of their brain, and cognitive training can improve this.
3. Children use different memory systems to ride a bike and recall a phone number.
4. Drinking less than six glasses of water a day seriously affects brain function.
5. Kids are better at learning when they are given data suited to their learning style.
6. Children have a Left or Right brain dominance and this, impacts on learning.
7. Boys' brains are hard-wired to be better at spatial awareness than girls' brains.

The answers are at the end of this chapter

In Summary

Now that you have a solid understanding of what NLP is and how it works, and more importantly how you can combine this knowledge with rules in your home, here are a few points to keep in mind:

Communication is always possible

No matter what you say and no matter what you do, you are communicating. When you think you're not saying a word, you're still communicating. Think about the last time you gave the silent treatment to someone. While you weren't talking, you were certainly communicating. Everything you do is a form of communication. Using NLP will help you ensure your communication is appropriate and productive.

Reality isn't always real

While you might think the world around you is straightforward, sometimes what you think is happening or what happened isn't necessarily accurate. What you need to remember today is that reality isn't just what happened, but how you interpreted what happened.

Responses matter more than what's said

You might say something to someone and not mean it, but their response matters more. If something happens, no matter what is said, the response to this occurrence is the important thing to keep in mind.

Flexibility is important

You might need to change the way you look at the world in order to be more effective and in order to help your child learn, grow, and be a success. The more flexible you can be, the more helpful you will be.

Constructive feedback increases success

While there will be times when things need to be changed, this does not mean that anything is "wrong". Instead, focus on the idea that feedback is a way to learn something new. If you never learned something wasn't working, you would continue to do the same thing again and again. You don't have to repeat old patterns and ideas when you understand how they're not working for you and those around you.

Not everyone is the same

True, it would be easy if there was a book that listed all of the rules you need to follow in order to create a certain result. But not everyone is the same. If you were to impose your rules on another family, that family might act differently and see different results from the actions. Instead, you need to accept the reality that your life is different from others.

True/False Answers

1. False
2. False
3. False
4. True
5. False
6. False
7. False

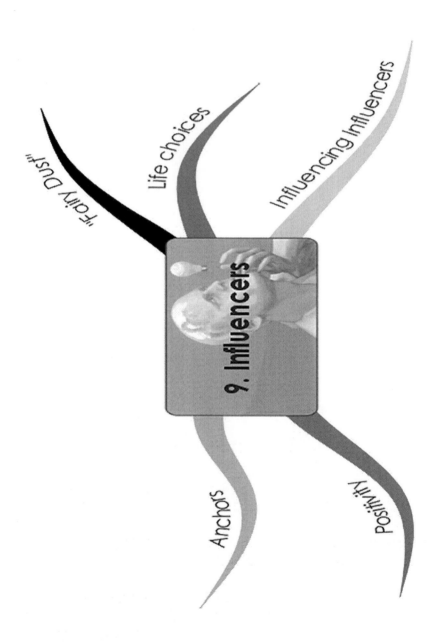

Chapter 9
Influencers

"When it comes to developing character strength, inner security and unique personal and interpersonal talents and skills in a child, no institution can or ever will compare with, or effectively substitute for, the home's potential for positive influence."
Stephen Covey

The Magic of Fairy Dust

Matt and his son Karl popped into a neighbour's house to collect a parcel that had been left there by the postman, and they were invited in for a cup of tea.

When they sat down Matt noticed one of the daughters, who was about five years old, was covered from head to toe in bandages. Matt can take it from here.

"She's got really bad eczema," the mum said.
"Is anyone working with her?" I asked.
"Well, she gets cream from the doctors."
"No, I mean working with her mind?"
Mum smiled and said that if there was anything I could do she would be very grateful. Karl smiled at me, "Are you going to fix her, Dad?" he whispered excitedly. "We'll see son, we'll see," I shone back at him, hoping that some of his magical faith in me would rub off on this tiny little girl.

I sat on the chair in the living room and recounted to the girl how a few months earlier, I was out walking with my two dogs Priest, a very elegant Staffordshire Bull-Terrier and Chip, a Yorkshire terrier who believes he is a lion.

Our walk was, at first, just like any other walk on any other day. We left the house and walked from the back gate, beside the railway lines and then into the tunnel, which took us from one side of the tracks to the other.

Sometimes, if you are walking in the tunnel, a train trundles past and you can feel excited and scared all at the same time.

Anyway, we were about half way through the tunnel, between getting darker and getting lighter, when suddenly the dogs started pulling on their leads and growling, which isn't like them at all. I looked into the darkness and there crouched down, hiding was a tiny little man. I put out my hand and he stepped onto it, so I carried him out of the reach of my dogs and into the light at the end of the tunnel.

"Thank you very much, sir," said the man who stood no taller than my little finger, in the palm of my hand.
"No problem at all," I replied casually, as if I did this sort of thing all the time.

"I would like to reward your good deed with some fairy dust," he beamed at me. "Fairy dust?" I responded somewhat bewildered. "I am a bit old to believe in fairies, my friend." The little man went on to explain that he was the king of the fairies and he would give me the fairy dust to prove it.

The little girl was hooked and waiting for what happened next, I hadn't thought beyond this point, so I excused myself for a moment and asked mum if she had a sheet of kitchen roll. I followed mum into the kitchen leaving the spell bound children to await the rest of my tale. Once in the kitchen I asked mum to put some pepper onto the kitchen roll and then I wrapped it up and put it in my pocket.

Returning to the chair, I explained how I only had a little bit of fairy dust left and I would be willing to leave it here with the family. I then went into great detail to explain how fairies would come during the night to reclaim their dust and how unlike the tooth fairy, who gives you money for an old tooth, they would grant wishes instead for each piece of fairy dust they collected. I then sprinkled a little bit of dust onto the little girls head.

"Now it may not be tonight or tomorrow night but certainly by the morning after the third night, the fairies will have been and your wish will be granted." Then Karl and I left.
Four days later I had two unexpected visitors to my practice. Mum and daughter who were both very happy as the little one had awoken on the third day without a blemish on her skin. And now in 2014 I am glad to say the magic still holds for what is now, a strong and healthy young woman.[54]

As the story above attests, while you might be the primary source of information your child accesses, you are not the only person in their life that will influence the way they think and the way they learn.

Your child doesn't just live in a bubble at home. Besides, by mastering the communication tools outlined in this book we can all learn to interact more effectively in the world around us.

It's a good idea to understand the ways in which others can impact your children as much as you do.

Influencing Greater Life Choices

You can have influence in any situation in life. Whether you are teaching your child a new subject or they are facing anxiety over a test you can help to clear away thoughts that might limit them.

You might influence them for better coping strategies in test anxiety, bullying, better communication, better grades and stronger family interactions. But you already know this by now. Why then should you want your influence to be extended into other parts of your child's life?

Congruency

If your child has an experience in one environment and then another experience in a different context that can lead to confusion about what they should be doing. As soon as one understands how the brain is interpreting information it receives; one now has conscious choice to act congruently or incongruently. Where there is no choice there can be no conscious awareness.

Increased effectiveness

When you continue to use the same practices in different contexts learners begin to see greater rewards from repetition. Instead of simply doing these practices when they are needed, learners behave and respond effectively and cognitively in the moment.

More inspirational people

The late personal development expert Jim Rohn said: "We are the sum total of the five people we spend the most time with". Look at your five. How have they influenced your thoughts, what you read, what you listen to and how you behave? Are you achieving similar success to that of your friends? Stop comparing and start progressing.

Influencing Influencers

How can we influence others to communicate more effectively? Robert Cialdini, the author of Psychology of Persuasion, gives us six principles of influence.[55] Cialdini identified these six principles by scrutinising what he called "compliance professionals"—salespeople, fundraisers, recruiters, advertisers, marketers, and so on. These are people skilled in the art of persuading and influencing others.

The six principles are:

1. **Reciprocity:** We usually aim to return favours and treat others as they treat us. Cialdini calls this reciprocity. This can encourage us to feel obligated to offer something to others if they have offered something to us.

2. **Commitment and Consistency:** Cialdini says we have a deep desire to be consistent. For this reason, once we've committed to something, we're then more inclined to go through with it. For example, you will probably be more likely to support a colleague's idea if you had shown interest when she first talked to you about it.

3. **Social Proof:** This assumes that if lots of other people are doing something, then it must be OK. And applies especially when we're feeling uncertain. We follow the crowd to feel safe.

4. **Liking:** Cialdini says that we're more likely to be influenced by people we like. They might be similar or familiar to us, they might pay us compliments, or they might engender trust.

5. **Authority:** Uniforms, job titles, white coats and even brands, cars or gadgets promote authority, and can persuade us to accept what these people say.

6. **Scarcity:** We tend to find things more attractive when their availability is limited, this seems to be driven by not wanting to "lose out". For instance, we might buy something immediately if we're told that it's the last one, or that a special offer is ending soon.

You have some influence over your child's environment so as Gandhi exhorts:

"Be the change that you want to see in the world".
Be the model for your children.

Parents

Parents, teachers, siblings, therapists, family members are all influential figures in a child's life. Though you might be "just" a parent, there are many other roles you will adopt for your child in order to support their development and progress.
Some of the shoes you will step into include:
- Coach
- Guide
- Care-Taker
- Mentor
- Sponsor
- Teacher
- Awakener

But what does all this mean and why is it important to know what role you're stepping into? Good questions. Let's continue to learn about how you as a parent or caregiver can be most effective.

Coach

You've already begun your work as a coach for your kids. And you've done a great job so far. There are plenty of ways in which a coach can progress a child, especially if they're also the parent or caregiver.

Instead of simply being a person who is there for a child, you can be the person who guides your child to an awareness of where they are now and what they need to do to progress no matter what might be happening around them.

Here are few of the ways in which a coach can support a child:
- **Work with building anchors**: Using the processes in this book, you will begin to create strong anchors that can be used to better influence emotional states, no matter how anxious the situation might be.
- **Help evaluate their lives**: Value where they are now (medal) and help them develop the criteria for progress (mission).[56] By focusing on what they are already good

at, and where they would like to go, you can begin to create a stronger purpose and direction for your child.

- **Question perceptions**: Since your child might see the world in one way, you can coach them to looking at the world in a different way. Instead of questioning why they feel they way they do, encourage them to question their own thinking and whether they might want to change things.
- **Use the different positions of thinking**: By using exercises like the one in which different hats are worn or the one where the child sits in different areas of the room, you can coach them to have different positions in their thinking, expanding their experience and their overall actions.

A coach is someone who is there to help a person progress. You might want to remember some golden rules when you step into the role of being a coach:

- If you're flexible, your child will also be
- Feedback against known criteria not a criticism
- You will need to build rapport before you begin to coach
- Every action your child takes is a learning opportunity

A coach is the role productive parents regularly adopt since this can create a successful working relationship.

Guide

When you want to help your child develop and progress, you don't always have to be the one to teach them everything. Instead, as the "guide on the side", you can make it easier for a child to find their own way.[57] You might have a map and different ways that you can coach them to the "right" way, but as the guide, you focus more on giving them guidance and encourage them to use the guidance in the way that makes the most sense to them.

A Guide will:

Encourage rapport with the child

You will show your child through example how to interact with another person.

Create new perspectives

Gently encourage your child to see things in a new way. This will help them to make their own decisions about how to proceed.

Work with the child's imagination

Children are naturally curious, by asking and encouraging your child to ask lots of questions, you can learn more about your child and they can learn more about themselves.

A guide is a role in which you step back and see what your child needs from you. You aren't telling them what to do, but you are giving them a few tools to see how they help. Since these tools are designed to be effective in any number of situations, your job is to simply get out of the way of the learning.

Caregiver

At the same time, sometimes, you just want to be the Caregiver. You might want to sit with your child and make sure they feel okay. This is a good role to take on when your child is dealing with something that is difficult for them to manage. They might need you to simply listen to them vent, without criticism and without any sort of lesson. You can sit with your child and:

Let them feel what they need to feel

You aren't going to tell your child to do anything when you allow them to experience their feelings. Instead, you might encourage them to label their feelings in even more detail.

Listen to them talk about their lives

You will want to make space in your day to listen to your child and encourage them to feel like they are heard. By communicating the way they do, they will feel safe. Your goal as a Care-Taker is to make sure your child feels safe when they are with you.

Mentor

Sometimes you might work with a child that isn't yours or you might want to create a little more distance for your child's growth. This is where the mentor role can be helpful. By taking the time to be a role model for your child, they will learn how to look at the world and they will be ready to try something new for their learning and for their growth. You might try the...

Museum of Old Beliefs

By letting your child move from place to place to learn what their beliefs might need to do in order to fall away or to change, you can help them see what they can do.

Encourage your child to act "as if"

When you allow your child to act as if they are already in the emotional state they want to be in, they can begin to understand the benefits of this state and work actively to get there.

Reframing

By introducing and practicing the idea of reframing, you will begin to establish a way the child can emulate when you do this for your own life.

As a mentor, you will create a space in which they see what the end result of their work with you might do.

Sponsor

A sponsor is someone who wants the very best for your child – both now and in the future. This is a role where you encourage your child to reach for their dreams.

In this role, you might help your child to uncover the things they really want to do with their life.
As a sponsor you will:

Figure out what motivates your child

When you begin to learn more about your child, you will begin to know what motivates them and how you need to talk to them in order to keep them motivated.

Build their self-esteem

When you listen to a child and you support their dreams, you are helping to build their self-esteem. By realizing they have dreams they want to fulfill, you will help them feel as though they will get everything they want in life.

Listen to them

It's important in every role—even more so as a sponsor—that you listen to your child as they begin to process their dream. No matter what they say or what they think they want to do, you need to listen and to encourage them to share their emotions about their dreams as well.

Visualise their dreams achieved

You may want to encourage your child to stop and to visualise what they want from their life. This may help them to better see the finish line. They can hold this image in their head making it more detailed as they learn more about what they want and they anchor into the success that comes with it.

With the sponsor role, you will need to be open to all of your child's ideas. When listening to their dreams, be sure to stay open to what you hear and be open to what they say.

You will find that the more you listen, the more they will be willing to tell you about what they want to do next. One of the most important things you need to do in the role of a sponsor is to make sure you have respect for the way your child sees the world.

This is a time for your child's true essence to be supported and understood in the now and in the moment. When you can focus less on how you see the world and more on what they see, you will be able to get an idea of what your child wants and what your child might also need from you.

Teacher

The teacher role is the role that many parents will fall into naturally. You want to share with your child what you see in an effort to help them break through any limiting ideas or beliefs they might have in their minds right now.

The more you can support and teach, the more the child will be willing to learn.

Some things a teacher will want to do include:
- The alphabet game
- Walking exercise
- The different hats
- The creative trio
- Getting reflective

Each of these exercises contain ways in which a child can challenge their own learning in order to find new and creative ways to solve problems. But it is the child's experience that teaches them. You will also want to make sure you keep in mind:

Children have their own reality

While you may not understand everything that a child does, realise they are still learning. The way your child interprets the world is something to learn and something to respect.

Children do what they do

A child will do the best they can with the resources they have available. The more resources they have, the better they will do. The fewer resources they have, the more they can learn.

Feedback is not criticism

While you might be given feedback in the role as a teacher, this should be formed and framed as ways to improve, not that the child is a failure.

Reflection

The very essence of learning is born out of reflection. Knowing where one is, knowing how one got to where one is and knowing what one needs to do to get where one wants to be. Though it can be tempting to think the teacher role is best left to teachers, instead, realise you can have a lot of influence as a teacher too.

Awakener

An Awakener is a role that encourages a child to look at their place in the outside world. When this happens, the kid is able to focus on their community, their family, and on others outside the home. As an Awakener, you may want to use these tools:

Question quest

Have your child go with you on a mini-vision quest to get the answer to a question they might have in their mind. Encourage them to walk in the woods or in another stimulating place whilst thinking about their question. See how many answers they come back with when using their surroundings for inspiration.

Introduce the idea of assumptions

When you are with your child, encourage them to be aware of assumptions about anything and everything. By introducing other ideas and noticing assumptions when they are used, you can begin to show your child that assumptions are not always "true".

Encourage creative thinking

If you are with a younger child, ask them about animals they like. Take one animal and ask your child to see how they might help with a problem they have. For example, if your child is having troubles with their history class, what would a hippo provide for them? How could the hippo help?[58]

When you are in the awakener role, the goal is to encourage the child to think outside of the box. The child will have more resources from which to draw, resources they may not have realised were available before.

When you are in this role, it's good to:

- Introduce your child to a larger world
- Offer resources to educate about the larger world
- Recognise your child can do more in the world

In this role, there are no limits to where a child can find knowledge or help. They can simply be in the world and enjoy all that the world might have to teach them. But please ensure they are made aware of potential risks, for example wandering off alone or with strangers and the general stay safe rules, for different contexts.

You can switch from role to role, as it seems fit. There is no one role that should be used in any given situation. Find a role to begin with and then move from role to role to see how your child responds.

You might find that these roles allow you to become an even better parent—and an even better person. Flexibility is the key.

Other Influencers

Teachers

When you send your child off to school, you may assume a teacher is going to have the child's best interests at heart. That may or may not be the case. When you're trying to work with your child in a certain way, it's a good idea to sit down with a teacher in order to talk to them about how you can support each other.

How teachers can help? Teachers are able to help in a variety of ways. Since your child might see their teachers more than they might see you, it's a good idea to begin to think about ways the teachers might be able to support that you're trying to instill in your child.

A teacher can:

- Encourage your child to develop effective learning strategies
- Promote a safe and inspirational learning environment
- Understand and apply the principles of rich feedback both for the learner and themselves
- Develop cognitive abilities
- Keep their toolbox current and well-practiced

When you notify the teacher of the emotional challenges the child is trying to overcome, they will be more alert to changes in their personality and in their behaviour.

This will help the teacher and the child begin to work together. A teacher can keep an eye out for things that might not be going as well as they might have liked.

The teacher will also be able to report back to you on progress. Together, you and the teacher can begin to work to help your child, especially when they are nervous about schoolwork or they have behavioural problems at school.

It might be a good idea to talk to the teacher about the things the child is learning specifically for the classroom and what subjects might have been causing troubles for them in the past.

Though the teacher may already be aware of these issues, they also may not. Learning this information from you and knowing the child is actively working toward resolving the issues, can help everyone understand the child's learning process.

How children can learn from teachers

Your child can learn at least as much from their peers as they do from their teachers. This provides opportunities for dialogue (talking with a purpose in mind), which is critical for them in order to construct meaning for themselves about their learning.

They can learn how to:

Reframe information

By reframing information they have received, children are able to see that every action can be the result of a positive intention, they are no longer threatened by the actions of others, including other students and teachers.

Get a different perspective

Teachers have a worldview too, they are individual human beings, they were once children and they continue to be learners.

Influence their state

Anchoring can happen anywhere, even in the classroom. With this tool, a child will be able to evoke to a positive emotional state, no matter what is happening around them.

A child is learning in the classroom in more ways than you can imagine. And while this might not seem to be the case when the teacher is not specifically teaching, the lessons can travel anywhere the child might be.

Siblings

If you're teaching one child something, it might be a good idea to extend the lessons to everyone who is in your family. Children who seem to be more flexible in the way they approach learning and experiencing the world can become your allies as you begin to create a new experience for another sibling. You can either ask the siblings directly to help you with the NLP lessons or you might want to teach everyone at once. When you do this, your child will see that NLP can work for everyone. They can begin to see the results of the techniques, especially when they can't see the results in themselves.

How siblings can help

The siblings in a family can be a great help when your child is beginning to learn and experience life in a new way. Siblings can:

Teach lessons

In the words of Lev Vygotsky: "If you want to learn something, teach it to someone. The one who does the talking, does the learning."[59]

Stand in for you

A child who is older might be able to do the lessons you want to teach with your child when you're not around. This will help to continue the learning and the growth of your child, even when you're not able to be there.

Practice lessons

When the children know the lessons, they can begin to practice them together. The alphabet game, for example, is one that everyone can do when mum and dad are not around.

Show the lessons in practice

You might also encourage the siblings to show the lessons in practice. For example, if an older child is having a tough time with math, they might work through this limiting belief and have the other child see how they do it.

Be a role model

Whether they try to be or not, older children will be role models for the younger children. Knowing this, they can endeavour to be positive role models at all times.

Focus on positive attitudes

Of course, siblings should be encouraged to be positive in the way they interact with others.

They should be encouraged to find positive intentions in everything that is happening in the family. Siblings can do a lot to help, especially when they're older. As they become older, they will be able to support each other and they will be able to teach even more lessons. Here are a few points to remember…

Progress takes time

Not all siblings are going to learn at the same rate that their sisters and brothers might. There are no contests in learning more about life and how to be a better learner, child or human being.

All learning styles have value

Some siblings will have one learning style while another might have another. No matter how they learn, there is something to be learned from different learning styles.

Siblings can be friends

Since siblings will be able to build rapport more easily with the tools they learn and because of their relationship, they will be more likely to create a stronger bond with each other.

Siblings have values to be respected

Everyone has the right to believe what they want to believe, even if it's difficult to understand. Siblings can find out what others think and value, helping to make them better companions.

Sibling experiences can provide anchors

When siblings are together, they can have positive experiences, which can then provide anchors for other life situations. When they are together, they can then remind each other of those positive feelings.

The siblings will be around each other even more often than a parent might be around a child. When they are actively supporting each other, focus on the idea that everyone is learning to be the best version of themselves, rather than one child needing "help", everyone will work together. And this might make your household a much nicer place in which to live.

Therapists

If your child is currently seeing a therapist, this mental health professional may want to find out what is happening at home. The more they can understand about a child, the more they will be able to build rapport with them.

Therapists will use the tools they are comfortable with to support your child in understanding their own unique model of the world. They are taught how to build rapport, how to speak to one's level, and how to assess the way a person thinks. The therapist might be the person who can help your child the most and help to support their new way of thinking most effectively. The therapist your child sees is already helping them with:

- Limiting beliefs
- Anxiety
- Worries
- Bullies
- Family issues, etc.

All of these issues are being worked on in the therapists' office, but they can be helped even more with the techniques you are learning from this book. The therapist can help by:

Assessing the progress

By knowing when the child began the work in this book, the therapist can see the changes that are happening. They can measure how the therapy is working.

Finding out the child's feelings about the tools

A therapist can also talk to the child about whether they feel better since they're learning new tools. They will be able to find out if the child is happier or if they feel that things aren't going well.

Working with key beliefs

If your child is working with certain limiting beliefs or with beliefs that are meant to take the place of limiting beliefs, let the therapist know. They will then be able to help the child understand what they are doing and how they are progressing.

When you talk with the therapist, set some time aside before your child's appointment. This way, you can quickly update the therapist on what is happening and what they can do to help support you in this endeavour.

How children can learn from therapists

Children are already learning a lot from their therapists, but they can learn even more.

How their emotions are affected

A child will be able to talk about their emotions, knowing that everything they say is right and valuable.

How their self-knowledge helps them

Your child will begin to see that everything they learn about themselves is a chance to learn how to progress.

How to change their minds

A child will begin to see with the therapist that changing their minds is possible and even necessary in some cases.

How to assess themselves

A child will look at the therapist and see the way that they are asking questions. They will be able to see the positive intentions behind this, which is going to lead to more productive sessions.

Your child's therapy will be even more effective when they begin to create new ways of thinking. The more they do, the more they will know, and the more they will learn about themselves.[60]

Family members

The family is always the assumed group that will want to help your child out. But sometimes, things can get sticky. Though the family wants to support your child in any way they can, they might also have troubles figuring out why you're doing what you're doing. They might have a different way of framing your situation and they might believe they can do better. While this might present a possible confrontation, this new way of working with your child might also present new possibilities for everyone. You will need to sit down with your family to have a heart to heart in order to begin the process of understanding each other's meanings.

How family members can help

Family members can help to support the process of your child's development by understanding what you are doing.

You can help them help your child by:
- Teaching a few tools to use
- Communicating with them frequently
- Modeling the practices you are teaching
- Encouraging more constructive communication

You might want them to be present when you are first showing your child some exercises. This will help to provide the model and it will help to show the importance of what you are trying to do.

You don't necessarily want to change what grandparents or other relatives are doing, but having them support what you and your child are trying to accomplish will help your cause.

Though this might be a practice that takes time, you can also look at this as being progress in action. And sometimes, progress takes longer than you might realise.

How children can learn from family members

Children are going to learn much from the family members they are around. Because they are learning to look at the world in a wider way, they can begin to see that their relatives can teach them more about how to see the world in new ways.

Your child will begin to understand that their relatives are able to process information in different ways and still come to the same conclusions.

Children can also:
- Learn how to build better rapport
- How to create stronger connections
- How to process information, holding the best intention for their relatives

Be aware! If you or your partner have any issues with your relatives, your child will pick up on it, so step up and be the best role model that you can.

How to Surround Your Child with Positivity

The truth is you aren't necessarily going to be able to shield your child from the negativity in the world. But you can certainly try to bolster the ideas that your child has learned. This will help them stay positive more often than not.

And what we do most often is what we will turn to when we're not thinking about it. This is going to help your child become more effective and it will allow them to be a positive light in the world. What an amazing thought!

Thoughts go everywhere

A good practice to encourage is to sit with your child each morning to listen to their responses. You might ask:
- What are you thinking about today?
- What might you want to change today?
- How can I help?

When you embolden your child to talk about their day before it begins, the can see when they might need to do some additional anchoring before they enter school or another environment.

They might realise that they are anxious about something, so they will need to access a non-anxious emotional state to help them persevere. You might also want to create a happy memory every day they can take with them. For example, you might talk to them about something happy as you are driving to school.

Each day, your child can associate happy emotions with being at school. This will allow them to have a positive state of mind when they walk in the door. Even if your child takes a bus to school, you can talk to them about happy things before they leave.

When they are already anxious about school, focusing on positive ideas and emotions before school, they can create a new connection and a new thought process that doesn't assume school will be difficult.

Your child can begin to see that she is able to influence her emotions and that she is able to create a new pattern for her day.[61] She can walk into the door of her school and know she is going to be ready to reframe anything.

Reframing is a particularly powerful practice to do first thing in the morning. Should you hear that your child believes something about a school event, you can ask them to describe it in more detail.

This will allow them to "vent" a bit about what they feel. Then you can begin to ask questions about what the event actually entails. This will allow them to focus on the "what" and the "how", rather than the "why".

You can also begin to question their assumptions in a non-confrontational way:
- What makes you think that way?
- What might you change?
- What can be changed?
- What are your options?
- What else could you do?

When you talk to your child about these questions, they can begin to dissect the thought more and they can begin to create a new pattern of thought. In the words of John Dewey, "A problem well put is a problem half solved."[62]

They may be able to reframe the thought that will encourage them to picture new options and new ways of thinking about the way they are handling a situation. In your conversation, you might be the coach or the guide that can help them begin to see that there are other ways of looking at something.

The more you practice this before school or before a difficult situation. Together, you and your child can come up with questions that help them access their thinking pattern. Each day, you can look at these questions and answer them.

The point is not to come up with clear answers to everything, but to instead encourage thinking things through in a productive way. After all, when you encourage new reframing of a situation, you encourage new thoughts, new actions, new ideas and new positive emotions.

Instead of looking at points your child brings up as "issues", you can look at them as topics of conversation that can be discussed. In that discussion, you will begin to uncover other ways to think about the topic.

The importance of anchoring

Anchoring becomes especially important for your child when you are trying to encourage a more constructive approach in their life. When you create solid anchors, you are able to access them in any situation. It is a good idea for your child to have anchors for any anxiety producing situation and also anchors for school, home, sports, friendships and so on.

Let your child practice drawing the learning from a range of different memories to apply to any situations that makes them anxious. Note: their interpretation of the situation causes the anxiety so helping them to realise this will be very beneficial.

Before any of these occasions, your child may want to think about a happy memory that happened in the past. They should see it in their mind, taste it, smell it, touch it and hear it. This idea should be solid in their mind, using their imagination to bring themselves back to that day or that moment.

When they do, they should think about what emotion they feel and how that made them feel in that moment. As they find themselves in a difficult situation, they can begin to access that other memory in order to bring them to a more productive state of mind.

Again and again, they can return to these images, making them stronger, and making the emotional content stronger and more effective.

Stop and really listen to them after the event to promote reflection. During this time, they might have emotions they don't know how to handle. While they might want to simply be mad or sad or frustrated, encourage them to think of a happy time in the same environment.

When they can have this emotion in their mind, have them stay in that spot and then think about what is frustrating them about their life. Ask them about what they could do and what they might want to do the next time they are in the situation.

They will be able to create a larger list of resources and possibly alternative actions. And while the situation might not be resolved, their response to the situation will be and they will be able to learn from what has happened.

Handling miscommunications

At times, when you are first implementing any new learning with your child, you might have some difficulties communicating. To avoid miscommunications be clear about the rules, remain nonjudgmental and really listen to them while remaining completely present. When you are thinking about talking to a teacher, for example, get clear in your mind all of the things that this person wants for your child. You might come up with a long list of ways this other person wants to help your child. This strategy works equally as well if you are a teacher preparing to talk to a parent. Always keep in mind that you are looking from a position of helping the child.

Handling issues

Sometimes, you might have issues that come up. The most frequent issues include:
- Different rules at different places
- Misunderstandings of goals
- Frequent negative talk
- Problems with child's new way of being

In the end, you can't change what others do, but you can change the way you perceive the issues. Instead of looking at these problems as a sign that you need to change your child's environment, turn these into things that your child can work out with their new tools. And they will.

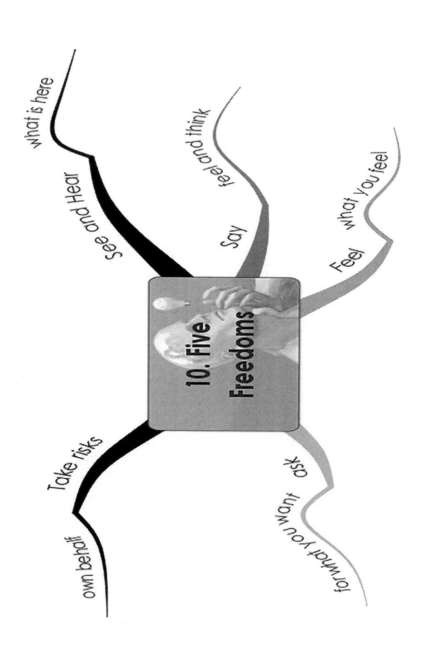

what is here

See and Hear

Say

feel and think

Feel what you feel

10. Five Freedoms

Take risks

own behalf

ask

for what you want

Chapter 10
Five Freedoms

"There is no single effort more radical in its potential for saving the world than a transformation of the way we raise our children."

Marianne Williamson

A Fishy Tale

Colin, a twelve-year boy, had been bullied by another lad at school and although he was the injured party, the school sent both boys home for a week to cool off. It was several months after the event that Matt eventually got to meet this likeable young lad. He can explain what happened next.

Mary, Colin's mum, was visibly distraught as she attempted to recount the tale. I interrupted her, immediately, explaining that one of the problems a child faces when they have been bullied, is the fact that you, as the parent won't let go of the problem, long after the kids are friends again. Please remember your child's map of the world is uniquely theirs and yours is yours.

The interruption of Mary, who was doing a very good job of keeping her son in the very state of mind that he didn't need, was just enough to allow Colin some breathing space. I asked him how it felt to feel really good and excited, like the night before Christmas, or on holiday or something that just makes you feel fantastic! As I said it, I lifted my energy and created an excited state for Colin and me to chat in.

"When I caught my first fish," he said.
"Wow! You've been fishing and caught a fish?" I encouraged
"Yep! All by myself, and I took it off the hook, without hurting myself."

I spent a few minutes to increase Colin's resourceful state, before I asked: "What happens if you get a really big fish on the line?" He grew about seven foot tall and said, "I can handle it."

During the few minutes that followed, I asked Colin to take his resourceful state into the "I was bullied once" state to notice what was different as he thought about it now. Colin grinned like a Cheshire cat, and said: "I can handle it." We chatted about times and places in the future where this confidence would really be useful for him. The rest as they say is history. The key is to create a really big positive resource state, and it will flatten the un-resourceful one.[63]

How to Develop a Whole Person

Virginia Satir was a well-respected family therapist who developed the idea of the Five Freedoms.[64] Based on NLP constructs, these pieces of knowledge can be used to help anyone to grow and learn. They can also help an entire family or workforce to feel safe in their environment and to begin to interpret their surroundings in the way that works best for them.

Some organisations choose to adopt these freedoms as a basic set of overall family rules. To ensure you can use these well, we will talk about what they mean and how they might look in a variety of settings.

Freedom 1

"The freedom to see and hear, what is here.
Instead of what should be, was, or will be."

When you encourage children to look at what is actually happening, you encourage them to avoid speculation and assumption.

Instead of a parent believing a child is going to go through the "terrible twos", they might begin to look at the child's present behaviours instead of thinking an age is when something is going to happen.

Instead of a teacher believing a learner is going to be disruptive during a lesson, they might begin to look at modifying their own expectations and give appropriate feedback.

The child might be encouraged to:
- Ask questions
- Think about different meanings and meanings about meanings
- Discuss what they find out
- Experience more things

Any child who has the ability to experience the world in terms of "what" and "how" is prepared for creating experiences and knowledge that are based in fact. When kids experience the world in this way, they do not have to create emotional anchors to certain situations. They can look at a situation for what it actually is.

This allows them to clearly create solutions or new directions. By following the idea of being able to look at the world in terms of what is there, assumptions are minimised. As a result kids will not take actions based on what they think they might know about a situation.

This creates a safe environment, as everyone can be counted on to talk about their experiences and not what they think their experience was. We all need to consciously engage our brain and senses to fully experience what is before us. This can be applied to everything from school, workplace, family, friends and relationships.

Freedom 2

"The freedom to say what one feels and thinks,
Instead of what one should."

When anyone speaks, they want to be able to be heard, but they also want to say what they need to say. Sometimes, people can ascribe to the unspoken rule that everyone should say only what they should say – not what they really mean to say.

This leads to problems with assumptions, again, and it causes a person to focus less on what they feel and think. They focus more on what they feel they should feel or think. This is confusing for anyone, and so they begin to negate their own feelings because they don't think their feelings are valid in the setting. Instead, it's a better idea to focus on encouraging those around us to express what he or she feels or thinks.

This encourages people to speak up for themselves and to begin to create a conversation that is completely accurate for their experience in the moment. When they are able to focus on what their experience actually is, they can begin to express more clearly and more often.

A child who might have troubles interacting with others may be feeling cautious as they think they need to say something in particular in order to be heard. In your home environment, make it clear that everyone will say what they think, and everyone will say what they mean. When this is the rule, this encourages us all to think creatively or differently. And that is a good thing.

Since everyone interprets the world in a different way, this allows the kids to feel their way is also valid. You might encourage this sort of thinking by asking your child:
- What do you think?
- What do you mean?

- What do you want to say?
- What do you want to share?

In every conversation, everyone should feel these questions are being asked of them. When they feel this way, their thoughts are heard and they are validated. Make sure everyone in the family has a time to speak in a conversation, and that they are heard until they feel they have been heard.

If a child has troubles with saying what they think they should say vs. what they really mean, encourage them to speak first so they cannot be influenced by anyone else. In time, they will learn to express themselves clearly, openly and honestly, so their viewpoint is open to criticism, without their person being criticised. As a result they will be more likely to speak for themselves when they feel they have something to contribute.

Let them know: I will always listen to what you mean and what you think.

Freedom 3

"The freedom to feel what one feels,
Instead of what one ought."

When your child feels something, they might not be able to describe it, but they can still feel it. In Satir's discussion, the feelings a child or any family member feels should be allowed to be thought, no matter what they might be.

When there is no judgment about thought, this will allow a child or anyone to be more open to talking about their feelings, in any way they feel is necessary. As the family begins to operate in this way, everyone will feel as though their feelings are respected. This supports everyone to have a right to feel what they want to feel, when they want to feel it and to express themselves.

In addition, when someone does feel something, they can share it in order to help work through a potentially difficult situation. For example, when two people are having troubles communicating they can express their feelings based on what they really feel, not on what they think the other person wants them to feel.

Why would a person only express what they think they ought to? There are plenty of societal rules that enforce this sort of behaviour. For example, when a boy is out in public and he begins to cry because he is hurt, he is immediately told that he shouldn't feel bad about what happened because it is not right to show those feelings.

When this happens, the boy gets the lesson that his feelings aren't right and that he needs to tuck them away. Over time, he might not know how to express his feelings in a positive way, which can lead to further troubles in communication and interactions with others, as well as with the family.

Instead, by fostering an atmosphere where one is able to express feelings when they feel them or when they want to share them, the environment becomes more open and you no longer feel like you need to hide your feelings.

The more you can practice not telling others what they should be feeling, the more they can support feelings when they are shared—no matter what they might be. Feelings are different with different people, and though some might not be very easy or they could be embarrassing in public, they are still valid for the person who feels them.

In the family, you should be with people you love and you should feel safe enough to share your feelings in any way you see fit. This should be possible without having to worry about what you "should" or "should not" be feeling at that time.

Freedom 4

"The freedom to ask for what one wants,
Instead of always waiting for permission."

A child who wants to go to the bathroom might wait for a parent to tell them they can go to the bathroom—with less than pleasant results. Instead of waiting for permission, children should be encouraged to ask for what they want when they want it. When they do this, they come to realise their need can be met instantly, so long as they take responsibility for naming their needs and being clear about what their needs are.

When one can talk about what one wants with those around them. They are able to discuss what their needs are, even when they are young. In addition, family members and teachers can listen to these needs and address them directly. It is too much responsibility to assume that someone else can speculate about what you might need, especially when you are able to ask for these things yourself.

Imagine a child who is able to ask for:
- Something to eat
- To go to the bathroom
- Help with homework
- Guidance with a problem

The more you are encouraged to ask for what you want from life, the more comfortable you become with asking without waiting around for someone else to help them and satisfy their needs. As a result the child starts to make a connection between taking action and satisfying their needs.

By addressing their own needs, kids can begin to respond to the needs of others as well. This does not mean that a child should always help someone else out, and this does not mean they will always get help when they need it, but they ensure they will get help by at least asking for it. When parents, siblings, caregivers and teachers also practice this lesson, they are able to create a culture of asking for help, support and guidance from each other.

Freedom 5

"The freedom to take risks on one's own behalf,
Instead of choosing to be only 'secure' and not rocking the boat."

One struggle many of us face in our lives is the feeling of not being able to take risks. We become risk averse. This may be because you have learned it's better to choose the safe route instead of trying something completely new and different.

John Overdurf gives this example in his foreword to Matt's book, The Saboteur Within:
One day B.U. is playing amongst his toys that are all around him on the living room floor. There's B.U. laughing, B.U. exploring, learning and playing, surrounded by all sorts of things that fascinate him and he is engaged. To B.U., this is complete freedom, fun, and creative expression. B.U. is a happy child doing what a child that age tends to do.

Meanwhile Dad is driving home from work. He's had an awful day. Before going to work, he opens some mail he didn't have time to open the day before. It's a late payment notice from the bank. He gets to work and his boss informs him that he will have to take on more work since the company had eliminated one of his support positions. The day is a blur. With hardly time to eat, he downs a double burger, extra cheese, and chips while in a meeting and later his digestive system is protesting. Traffic is a mess. By the time he gets home, he is irritable and on edge. Spent. It won't take much to set him off. He opens the front door and sees "the mess" in the living room. He bellows, "Clean up this mess! Now... What's wrong with you? You should know better!"

All of a sudden, completely unexpectedly, B.U. the "free child" becomes "scared child". There are no filters to "make sense" of what is happening.

B.U., taking it all in, doesn't yet have the presence of mind to think, "Oh the old man must have had a bad day at work and has a nasty case of indigestion. You know he should learn to be more assertive and also watch what he eats." No way! Instead the message is imprinted, stamped into his neurology: Dad's voice, tone, words, and look on his face, and now feeling free is glued together with fear. In his brain these neural networks are being wired together.

No logic here. Just simple time and place. Literally these two very different emotional states become wired together. This is one of the most basic proven principles in neuro-science: Neurons that fire together, wire together. We know the brain wants to make things automatic as soon as possible.

So days later when Dad comes home, the last thing B.U. wants to do is see that look on Dad's face and hear that voice tone. He learns to be on-guard and vigilant when Dad comes home from work. This becomes automatic and starts to generalise to other situations that are similar. As time goes on, he feels scared when he does things he really likes doing, but doesn't really know why. It's that "waiting for the other shoe to drop" feeling. Now B.U. is all grown up, but he has one big issue: he can't really be himself. Every time he thinks about doing something where he's free to express himself – he gets scared something bad is going to happen.

Now that he is an adult, he can come up with "good adult reasons" why this is the case, but actually he has no idea how or why it happens. Nor does he realise how much it is holding him back. His unconscious is just doing what it learned to do. This response is automatic and wired in. His unconscious now functions as the saboteur within. This reaction is not what B.U. wants, but it happens persistently and predictably. Once again, it was an adaptation that worked before, but now it no longer fits the context.

To B.U., it's time for a change. The good news is the unconscious mind knows how to learn quickly and make the learning automatic. The new ways of being can become as permanent as the limitations once were. If we were to operate with the idea that risks are acceptable, what might happen, I wonder?

- Could each person learn more?
- Could each person experience more?
- Could each person establish his or her own uniqueness?
- Could each person know they were supported?

When a person accepts that everyone is able to take risks and is able to create a new way for themselves, they can be more open about their dreams, hopes and fears. Sometimes dreams don't sound realistic, after all. But they are still valid and still something that should be encouraged. If one has a strong feeling about something, one should be encouraged to take action and learn from the feedback.

They should still feel they can have a go. Freedoms—that's what these are. By establishing more freedom in your life, you will be able to improve communication, allow for more growth and you will strengthen your own self-worth and that of those around you. Enabling you to face life's setbacks with the resilience needed to weather the storm.

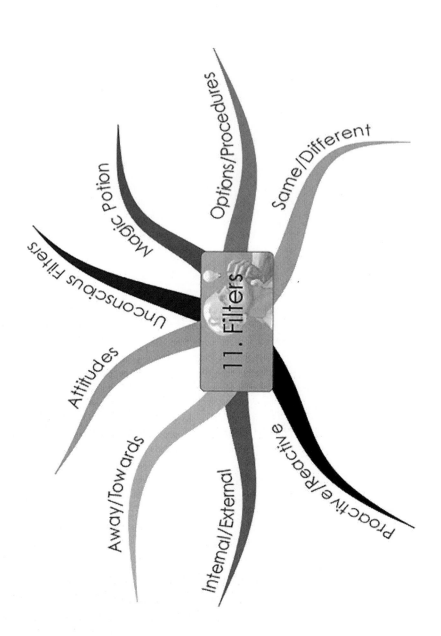

Chapter 11
Filters

"Live so that when your children think of fairness and integrity, they think of you."
H. Jackson Brown, Jr.

A Magical Potion for Any Notion

This is a mad idea that Matt dreamt up when his boys were young and it only works with the spoon in the cup, which he will explain at the end. Over to him.

When your child is growing up it is too easy to reach for the medicine cabinet and unleash the Calpol every five minutes. So one particular evening our youngest boy was complaining of having a headache; this was the third night in a row, which meant that my wife Sonya and I were very tired. As I'm sure you're only too aware, if the kids don't sleep, you don't sleep. Well, the trusted Calpol didn't seem to be having any effect on the little lamb, so I told him that I would have to give him some of the grown up's medicine.

I explained that it was very strong and he would probably be fast asleep within twenty minutes after taking it, or twenty-five minutes at the very most, and he would certainly have a good night's sleep beginning in the next half hour. The conversation above presupposes something is going to happen to the child after they have taken the medicine and even gives a time frame for this to happen. Now, the extra, below conscious part of the deal, comes as the child drinks. Because, by drinking the medicine, they are unconsciously accepting the presupposition, that they will fall asleep within the next half hour.

I would explain to our boys that the medicine was specially made for me because I couldn't swallow tablets and it was tasteless so that I could drink it easily. The set up here is very important, you have to get your first aid box out and ham it up a bit!

Here is the magical part, you fill a cup with cold water and then go to the medicine cabinet and pretend to add something, stir it vigorously with a spoon. Hand the cup to the child leaving the spoon in. When the child takes the cup you say, "Oops!" and take the spoon out of the cup. Hey presto! You have created a magical medicine that can be used for any minor growing problems your child might encounter. It can also be used to conquer nightmares as it gives the patient super powers in their dreams, giving them a really good night's sleep.

The key to all of this is of course the spoon. When you stir the water, it creates the illusion that there is something in it that needs to be stirred so that it can dissolve. Just in case the child doesn't hear you stirring it, you leave the spoon in the cup and take it out as you hand it over. Please be fully aware that your child can read you like a book, so understanding how he or she is filtering information will be very helpful for you.[65] A presupposition is an unstated or covert assumption, which may be verbal or non-verbal.

Meta Programs

Filters or Meta programs are based on the original work of Neuro-Linguistic Programming (NLP) founders Richard Bandler and John Grinder.[66] Shelle Rose Charvet points out, "There are over sixty different distinctions for identifying the things to which people were paying attention or ignoring, how they evaluated different situations and made decisions."[67] Below, we offer you an insight into some of these unconscious motivation and attitude drivers.

Attitude

What is attitude? While we think this is under our control, it's really a complicated process. And most of the time, it's completely unconscious. We think we're acting in one way, but the things we are saying might come across differently because of our attitude.

Think about it. Here's an example:
Anna wakes up in the morning and thinks the day is going to be horrible. Everything she does, she finds some fault in it. When she gets to school, she thinks all of her assignments are going to be impossible, so she doesn't do her work or she doesn't try very hard. After all, what's the point in trying if you know you're going to fail?

As she talks to her friends, she complains about what is happening and her friends think she's being too angry, so they leave. This makes Anna's mood even fouler.She goes home and grumbles to her parents who also think she's being a little too grumpy, so they send her to bed for her attitude.

While Anna might have been able to shake this bad attitude off, what she might not have realised was all of the consequences of her attitude. Because she looked at the world as though everyone was out to get her, she began to experience that experience.

"Like attracts like". When you think certain things, you attract certain things. When you're unable to change your attitude, you can begin to attract things you don't want in your life. And your child can easily learn this lesson too. But since your attitude is unconscious most of the time, how can you change what you can't control? Well, you can.

Different attitudes cause us to:
- View things differently
- Respond to situations differently
- Take different actions
- Be motivated in different ways

After this section, you will begin to learn the different ways in which your child might be motivated. By learning these ways, you will be able to use the right words to help them see they can be successful. And you can learn how to motivate a child who may be having troubles getting motivated.

A right attitude?

One way to begin to change your attitude is to think about your attitude not as something that is wrong or right. That will cause you to start thinking that certain emotions are bad. And they're not. Everyone has a bad day, but that doesn't make them a bad person. Instead, try to find the best possible reasons for everything that's happening in the world around you. And encourage your child to do the same. If a car is speeding in front of you, and it cuts you off, don't yell or scream in front of your child. Think about saying aloud, "Wow, that person must have an emergency to take care of. I hope everything is okay."

You can come up with a new attitude, just by looking for the best intentions in everything around you. This doesn't mean you're making your attitude "good" or that your attitude was "bad", it just means you need to focus on changing your attitude to make the world what you want it to be. You need to look for ways to bring in more positivity.

Positive, Positive, Positive

You can have a more positive outlook on life, no matter what is happening around you.

Think about positive reasons

Whenever you or your child is in a situation that is less than positive, think about things that could be positive about it. If you're in a long line, talk about how great it is that you can talk to each other for a longer period of time.

Rewrite the story

If each day of your life is a story, think about ways that you can rewrite it. The more you rewrite your story, the more you can see that things can be changed as soon as you change them. Children especially will enjoy the idea of changing the way they think about the world around them. They can sit down at the end of the day and think about how they might rewrite the story of the day so they don't feel badly about it.

Be the hero in your day

If your learner is told they are the hero that can save their day, this can reframe their experience. Talk to them about how they can look at their life as though they are a hero. What can they do in order to create a new and a better experience? How can they "save" their day?

Think of the other person

Each day, look around to see who you can help. This creates a more collaborative way of thinking and a way of beginning to create a new way of looking at the world. Instead of simply thinking of what they need, your kids can look to see what others might need around them and how different their life views or experiences might be.

Take care of your needs

In order to make sure that you can stay positive, it's a good idea to take care of your needs first. This will help you to create a solid foundation from which to use an anchor or to move in a new direction. If you're happy, then you can stay positive.

Focus on what you can change

When your kids are frustrated by the world around them, it's a good idea to challenge them to think about what they could change. If they look at what they can change, they will be able to take action.

Express your feelings

Of course, when your child is having troubles in their life, they should be able to express their feelings, no matter what they are. This will allow them to feel like they are being heard and that their feelings matter. When this happens, they will be able to focus on more positive things around them.

Being positive is a practice that takes practice. The more that you can focus on being positive with your children the easier it will be for them to be positive as well.
Positivity is infectious and it is something worth spreading around. But there are more attitudes that fall within this ideal positive spectrum.
Knowing what attitudes your child might have (and which attitudes you may have), can help you both better understand the other.

Away versus towards

Figuring out what your kids' attitude might be in their lives will help you to connect with them in a stronger way and it will allow you to create an environment in which they can be supported in every way possible.

When you think about your children, you need to determine whether they are motivated by goals or achievements or if they are motivated by avoiding the things that might bring them pain.

As you understand this, you will begin to understand what it means for your children to be in the world. They will begin to feel supported since you understand what and how they are perceiving the world.

Away from

Children who move away from the things in their lives, which might cause them pain will do everything they can to avoid this pain. They might simply avoid the situation or they might take actions to not be involved.

These kids might use words like:
- Steer clear of
- Prevent
- Eliminate
- Solve
- Fix
- Prohibit
- Avoid

Of course, these words can also be used by adults in life, and often is used more frequently by adults than younger people. These are people who are focused on seeing what is wrong with a situation. Though this might not seem to be a positive way to interact in life, it might also be exactly what your kids need in order to get on the right track.

Think about it, when you talk to your children about something that is bothering them and you use the language they would use, they will feel the rapport grow between you. When this happens, you will begin to see that your children works with the way they perceive the world and they begin to create solutions that work the way they think.

They look for ways to:
- Steer clear of problems
- Prevent issues
- Eliminate pain
- Avoid trouble
- Solve troubles
- Fix what's broken
- Prohibit events that might cause pain

One of the most common examples of this sort of attitude is the situation in which a person feels they cannot solve a problem because they feel there are too many things to eliminate. They feel overwhelmed and instead of handling the issue, they might end up avoiding it completely. While this might be a way for them to handle the situation, it can also cause a child to have more issues as a result.

Instead, you may want to work with your child to see what they are doing. You can create motivations that not only work within their framework, but also in the opposing framework—toward.

Toward

Those who are focusing on moving toward a solution because they see a goal being met or an achievement being made are commonly older. You, for example, might not see a problem as something that needs to be fixed. Instead, you might find ways that you can make this something you can move toward.

You might use words like:
- Attain
- Accomplish
- Achieve
- Get
- Rewards
- Results
- Goals
- Outcomes

All of these words focus on the idea that when something is done, then something else is achieved. This sounds more positive, because the person who is speaking is taking an active role in the way they are engaging with their life. They aren't moving away from the things that are complicated—they are moving toward solutions.

When you have a child like this, you might do better to be a parent who is following an "away" mindset, since the child will be able to learn about the possible problems in their ideas. This will help them have a larger picture of what is happening.

Parents, caregivers and teachers who tend to have a "toward" mindset and who have children who also have a "toward" mindset may have to think about how they communicate with each other since the adults may be focused on goals of their own. And they might not listen to the goals of the child.

"Toward" kids are clear in what they want. They are often achievers and those who do well in life. However, having the balanced perspective of what they might want to avoid is going to help them further their goals even more.

Internal – External

You may have already noticed that your kids are motivated more by their own internal drive. They are driven by something inside of them that makes them try to do more and to achieve more.

On the other hand, a child (as well as an adult, of course) can also be motivated by the external cues that show they are successful. These are learners who want constant feedback.

Where can you fit in?

What is Internal?

An internally driven learner will work on something because they want to work on something. They have an inner passion that allows them to focus on the things they want to do and it doesn't matter what anyone else thinks.

They will, however, have troubles hearing negative feedback. Since their process is internal, they aren't thinking about the concerns of others. All they think about is what they are doing.

They might:
- Create a story
- Write a play
- Organise something
- Build something
- Manage something
- Be a person who's off in the corner, content with themselves

Now, the "internal" child will be able to create things on their own. They want to do what they want to do because, well, they want to do it. The child will be singularly focused in many cases and might not even notice what's happening in the

world around them.
That's just the way they are. They might even focus on a new project and get outside opinions, but they will make the final decision on what to do by looking inside of themselves. "Internal" kids are able to focus, but they also have troubles accepting direction from others who are outside of them.

While they might need the direction or they might need the assessment of possible issues, they are not necessarily going to be as receptive as you might think they should be. This can be tricky.

But they can be motivated by phrases like:
- I need your advice
- I need your opinion
- You know what's best
- Only you can make that decision
- It is up to you in the end

When you allow the child to feel as though they have the final say in what they are doing, they are going to be more motivated and they are going to have a more positive attitude. Remembering that this type of kid wants to feel their internal process is validated is the key to success.

What is External?

Those kids who are focused on the external motivators are those who want to hear what others think. They might not start a project or use an idea they have until they are sure others will enjoy it. These children (and adults) have ideas, but they're not going to think they're valid until someone else tells them they are.

These children might:
- Want to perform
- Share their ideas with others
- Discuss with others

- Be with a lot of friends
- Be popular
- Be outgoing
- Be interested in what you think of what they do

A learner who is motivated by external cues is going to seek out the approval and the acceptance of others. Even if they think they have a good idea, they will not necessarily follow through unless they think others will accept it. This child may come across as needing a lot of attention and needing a lot of support when they are tackling important projects. You can "external" kids with words and phrases like:

- Your hard work will pay off
- You will be recognised
- Others will think highly of you
- According to experts
- Your teacher, therapist or family members will be pleased

You might want to look for outside ways that your child's efforts can be validated—and not just by you. Yes, it's important for you to point out that the work of your child is good and that it is praiseworthy, but when there are external motivations – i.e. honour roll—they will be feel like their work is with merit. If you are a parent, caregiver or teacher who is more "internal" than "external", it can be a challenge for the learner to feel like their work is worthy. They need to hear that they are doing well, and you simply may not think of this as something that's important.

Conversely, when an "internal" child is praised by an "external" parent, it can make them feel like their internal process isn't appreciated. Not sure what your child is? Ask them how they know they did well on a test. An "internal" child will talk about whether they feel they did well. And an "external" child will talk about whether they got a good grade.

Proactive – Reactive

You already know what it means to be proactive but reactive in "meta program speak" means that a person likes to analyse and consider the situation and waits for others to initiate action.

Proactive

A child that is proactive is someone who is motivated by avoiding problems to a certain extent. They are interested in getting ahead of others because they know they will gain from that action.

They know that when they are proactive, they can:
- Avoid problems
- Do something no one else has done
- Lead others
- Start something exciting
- Jump into new situations
- Take charge of the situation
- Influence others
- Motivate others

When you talk to a child who is a proactive, they will be most affected by phrases like:
- Go for it!
- Why wait?
- Take charge!
- What are you waiting for?
- Just do it!

These phrases are active and allow the kid to feel like they are moving in a positive direction. Proactive children are going to do what they want to do because they want to do it.
At the same time, many people who are motivated by the idea of being proactive don't think about the feelings of others.
They're only concerned with what they can do. Because of this,

they might step on toes along the way. They might be the ones who do things without thinking and then have to go back and redo things because they weren't done with thought. A person like this might:

- Be fidgety
- Want to do more and more
- Be in control, so they speak with authority
- Use shorter sentences with active verbs
- Have troubles sitting still

This is a person with energy to spare and they want to use it right now!

Reactive

Someone who is reactive is not necessarily the opposite of proactive, but they might be someone who waits before they act. They are motivated to think, think and think some more. Reactive children might respond to phrases like:

- Let's think about this
- Analyse this
- We need to understand this better
- Consider these ideas

Engage the fact that this kid wants to learn more when they are involved in something. Allow them to look at all of the angles of a problem—which is something a proactive child might not do. At the same time, the problem that can come up for a reactive child is that they are so focused on information gathering that they might forget completely about taking action. They might also take action too late.

You can see if a person is reactive by listening to the way they speak to you and with others. They use a number of conditional words like could, should, might, may and would. These words show there is still some thinking to be done, even if from your perspective they are ready to do something.

In order to motivate a reactive child, you might need to:
- Create time limits for decisions
- Limit the resources available
- Create a time for action

When you begin to define the time in which the deciding needs to be done, the reactive learner will be able to streamline their thinking process and get ready to act. Those parents, caregivers and teachers who are more proactive will help to engage the reactive child, while reactive parents, caregivers and teachers might have troubles seeing that their child isn't considering all of the possibilities.

Options – Procedure

If your child appears to want to play by the rules, they might be motivated by what happens if they don't follow them. Or they might simply be motivated by the idea of rules. Some children and adults are motivated by that which is concrete – rules, procedures and the likes. Others are motivated more by options. They are seen as being more creative and being more open. So how can you motivate these two sets of children?

Opinions... Options...

When your child is always looking for a new way to do things, you have a child that is motivated by opinions and options. He wants to know everything that's out there in an effort to try to find a new way of doing something he needs to do in his lives. Whether he's trying to solve a math problem or he's looking for a new outfit, he wants to try something that's new and exciting, no matter what the consequences might be. Children like this will be motivated by phrases like:
- Another option is
- Break the rules
- What are the alternatives?

- Expand your choices
- Possibilities
- Flexibility

The parent who is more flexible in nature will have a fun time with a child who is thinking and is motivated in the same way. They are going to spend hours working on finding the new possibilities and options in a problem. However, there are downsides to being a person who is motivated by the many options that are available in the world. Though this seems to be the more creative type, this can lead to other issues.

- They bend the rules
- They break the rules
- They get into trouble more
- They create rules and then don't follow them

Another potential issue is that you might have a child who is so interested in options that they become unpredictable. No one quite knows what they're going to do—not even them. This can present issues most often in the school or some other formal setting.

...Or procedure?

A kid who is interested in following the rules is one who is praised most by parents, caregivers and teachers. After all, they want to follow the rules. They feel safe when they are looking at the rules and checking them off in their head. They know they are doing the acceptable things and they don't worry about getting into trouble.

They use words and phrases like:

- Rules
- First
- Then
- A proven way
- The correct way
- Tried and true guidelines

Children like this feel they are best to follow the rules that are already in place. Whether these kids think these rules are better, that can be debated. But they will follow the rules and they might not think about anything creative outside of those rules. This can cause them to forget about other options, which might exist in relationship to solving a problem. For example, if they get stuck with solving a problem, they might not do anything since the options they understand aren't in the rules. They may just give up.

In order to help support a child who enjoys the rules:
- Have clearly defined rules
- Give clear instructions
- Establish a routine
- Encourage following of guidelines

This child will not be settled in an environment where they are not sure what is expected of them. If you are a procedures-oriented parent, you will be able to relate to a child of the same motivation style. But an opinions-oriented parent might have troubles creating rules for a learner, telling them to think things out instead. Another way to help a child is to show them there are alternative ways to look at things in their life. Even if they don't think they will work.

Sameness – Evolution – Revolution

Finally, there are children who might fall into one of three motivation or attitude categories:
- Sameness
- Evolution
- Revolution

Within these categories, you find many children. These children thrive on things staying the same, things improving or things changing. If your child is one who is comfortable in these situations, you can help to make them feel more comfortable and you can help them to use the motivations they have to do more in their life.

You can ensure your children are able to feel as though they are at home, no matter where they are.

The Idea of Sameness

A kid who does not want things to change is someone who thrives on sameness. Same routine. Same clothing. Same house. This is not to say they are completely against the idea of change, but they might want to experience change so slowly that they don't even realise it is happening. This is a child who decides what works for them and doesn't want that to change at all. They are comfortable so long as they know what to expect and what might happen next.

They use phrases like:
- In common
- The same
- It's just how it is
- Like before
- It's just the way I am

When you hear these words, you might want to keep in mind that those who do not like change simply need change to happen in a way that's comfortable for them. They might not want to change because they are afraid things will not be as great as they are right now. You will need to make sure you change things slowly for your child who is concerned with sameness. Or you need to make sure you are keeping some things precisely the same so they have some measure of sameness in their life:

- Have a routine
- See the same people
- Encourage your kid to decorate her room
- Take the same driving routes

While change is inevitable, when you can try to keep things the same, you will help this child. When change does have to happen, you might want to point out the new ideas and the structures that are similar or the same to what they are used to. This will help them feel more at ease.

The Idea of Evolution

A child who is interested in things improving, is one who is open to the idea of evolution. They want to experience better things and similar but extra ideas. They might not feel they can settle on just one idea. They want evolution in their life and when things are too structured, they can begin to feel restricted. This child might respond to phrases like:

- Let's see if you can improve on what you have done
- Can you do even better?
- Completely different
- It's almost the same
- Things are similar to...

The Idea of Revolution

This child wants to try out new things and to create major changes in their life more often than they want to stay the same. Children like this want to hear from you that they are learning something new and exciting.

If you want to support this sort of motivation in your child, bring in new ideas and ask them what they would want to change in their experience now.

This child might respond to phrases like:

- This is totally new!
- This is radical!
- Let's try something different
- Everything has to change
- You are a one off / unique

Learning Journal

It can help to keep a record of the attitudes your child has and the motivations they have. Together, you can begin to keep track of what they want to know, how they know, and what they want to do with this knowledge. This can also help to track what they have already done and what they can still do next.

How to Start a Journal

Starting a journal can be a simple process of writing down the ideas a child has or the way they approach situations in their life. When they write these down (or you write them down), you can begin to understand what your child needs in order to feel supported. They might create the journal themselves, decorating it in order to make it their own. Or they can choose a journal that is simple and plain. Beginning the journal can be as simple as buying one from the store and seeing how it can help you and your child see what is happening in their internal landscape.

Journal practices to use

Here are some practical ideas to help you get the journal started:

Write daily

The more the journal is used, the more it can be used to learn from the child. A daily practice of writing in the journal is the best way to ensure everyone benefits in some way.

Write during learning processes

As a child is learning something new or is interested in a new idea have them write in the journal or you can make an entry about their process.

Write new ideas

Sometimes, a journal is just a great place for a catchall for ideas that a child has. This can help keep them in one place where they can refer to them again.

Create goals and plans

If a child wants to work on certain things in their life, they might want to use the journal to write down those goals and the steps they need to take to get there.
You can use the journal to document the way your child thinks and what this means for your child's development.

Looking back, you can find trends in the child's learning and spot ways you could help more or ways you might want to step back from helping as much.

Children
From The Prophet

"Your children are not your children.
They are sons and daughters of Life's longing for itself.
They come through you but not from you.
And though they are with you, yet they belong not to you.
You may give them your love but not your thoughts,
For they have their own thoughts.
You may house their bodies but not their souls,
For their souls dwell in the house of tomorrow, which you
cannot visit, not even in your dreams.
You may strive to be like them, but seek not to make them like
you.
For life goes not backward nor tarries with yesterday.
You are the bows from which your children as living arrows
are sent forth.
The archer sees the make upon the path of the infinite, and
He bends you with His might that His arrows may go swift and
far.
Let your bending in the archer's hand be for gladness.
For even as He loves the arrow that flies, so He also loves the
bow that is stable."
Khalil Gibr

Conclusion

"If you want your children to be intelligent, read those fairytales. If you want them to be more intelligent, read them more fairytales."

Albert Einstein

Honour the Gift

Once upon a time, in a valley, far, far away, there lived a farmer. One fine, sunny day in June he awoke early, as farmers do, and decided to go for a hike across to the top of the nearby mountain, so that he could simply enjoy the view. When you look out into your world it's very easy to not see things that are familiar to you; your mind can hallucinate that nothing is changing, when really nothing can stay the same. It's your eyes that get old and that is why our farmer decided to take a look at everything with fresh eyes, as if for the first time. Children do this all of the time, everything is new and exciting.

The climb took longer than the farmer had expected and so it was, that several hours later than anticipated, he arrived at the top. He looked out on the valley below and was very pleased that he had kept going, even though the voice in his head had been telling him to stop and turn back, as it was too hard.

The farmer chuckled to himself because he had overcome the voice and rose to the challenge. After resting for a while, it was time to descend and it was here that he happened upon a bird's egg. The farmer guessed it might be an eagle's egg but since it was just sitting there, he figured that he could take it home and see if the chicks would hatch it. So, with the egg packed safely in his backpack, the farmer began his journey home.

As soon as the farmer arrived at the chicken coop he placed the egg under a broody hen and as luck would have it, a few weeks later a very healthy baby eagle hatched and wandered around, wide eyed, staring at the world around him. The other chicks treated him like he was just the same as them and so the eagle grew up believing he was a chicken.

The eagle learned to do everything chickens do: it clucked, scratched in the dirt for crumbs and worms, flapping its wings irately, flying just a few feet in the air before coming down to earth in a pile of feathers and dust.

This bird believed resolutely and absolutely that it was a chicken, even when, one afternoon when it looked up and actually saw an eagle gliding effortlessly, high in the sky, majestic and awe inspiring; he could not see himself as being or having the same abilities as this beautiful, graceful bird. Then one day, a stranger happened by and talked for a while with the farmer.

The stranger's voice rang with many tones, inflections and accents, which would attest to him being well travelled. He was, in fact, a wizard returning to his home in the north and would be willing to share some of his tales in return for a nice meal. The farmer was delighted to have such an esteemed guest and he spent the next few days, just listening to the Magi, who told the most entrancing stories.

Every now and then, he would glance inside the pages of his notebook and remind himself of the key ingredients to this tale or that one. The wizard took a liking to the farmer and within his incantations he weaved a learning spell, so that, as he listened, his mind would open up to brand new ways of seeing the world.

Spells sound like normal words to Muggles or none magic folk but they are really powerful devices for shaping perceptions, meanings and experiences. Therefore, a conversation with a sorcerer is apt to be multi-layered and dreamlike with rich interpretations, ready to transmogulate into some new word or meaning in an instant.

One particular account that the farmer was impressed by was when a large wolf tried to attack him up in the mountains. The wizard, instead of using a charm or spell or even a weapon to defend himself, simply hurled his arms in the air and ran towards his attacker yelling as loud as he could. The wolf stopped dead in its tracks, turned around and ran off. "Because," the Magi explained, "It's when you do the unexpected thing that you cause a lot of rearrangement in a person's thinking."[68]

The next day the farmer woke unusually late and his visitor was, by now, long gone. As he leaned over the fence, gazing at nothing at all, he saw for the first time, with new eyes, the eagle. He knew what he had to do And so it was that the farmer learned all he could from a curious book his guest had left behind, about how to develop and communicate with the eagle.

It would take a while for the farmer and the eagle to adjust to this new way of being together, but little by little the eagle learned to raise its head, to stretch its wings and even to eat food that was more befitting the wants and needs of such a regal bird. Much to the disdain of the other chickens, who thought he was weird and that he was no longer one of them.

It then came to pass, that one fine, sunny day in June the eagle beat its powerful wings and ascended. Soaring high above the trees, effortlessly climbing, on the updraft of the warm air. Within moments, he was able to be free from the nagging of the conforming chickens, who were compelled to obey the law of right and wrong. The eagle was now acutely aware that, the only one true law is that which leads to freedom.* "I am flying!" he yelled. "I am free!"

The farmer, now far below heard the sounds of the eagle and he knew all was good. He never forgot how proud he felt seeing the eagle taking its rightful place and he would one day retell the story in his own way to others.

It is our hope that you use the tools within this book to help you understand your child and perhaps the child inside of you too. Many of the passages can be reread at various times, and we would encourage you to do so, as they may just have deeper meanings and create even more connections for you and your child.

We do not profess to know all of the answers to the specific challenges you may be having with your child, as there is no right or wrong. But we do know that applying the tools will help you to make your family happier and that's a good start.

Ultimately this is a journey, and this book a guide to which you can refer back to, in the same way you can check a map during a long road trip. Even if you have just applied one of the principles, that you have gleaned from reading the book and it helps your child be more successful and makes your home life more fun, then that is excellent. If you are able to incorporate several of the strategies, then you are awesome… Enjoy the journey.

Further Training and Development

The authors offer a wide variety of training, which is aimed at personal and professional development.

You can contact them via their website www.matthudson.com or email info@matthudson.com.

References

[1] Rosen, S. (1991). My Voice Will Go With You. New York. W. W. Norton & Company, Inc. p113-117.

[2] Grinder JT, Bandler RW. (1975).The Structure of Magic. Palo Alto, CA: Science and Behaviour Books.

[3] Chomsky, N. (1957). Syntactic Structures. Mounton, The Hague.

[4] Seligman, MEP (1998). Learned Optimism: How to Change Your Mind and Your Life: A. A. Knopf.

[5] Frederickson B (2009). Positivity. Crown Archetype.

[6] Burkeman O. (2013). The Antidote: Happiness for People Who Can't Stand Positive Thinking: Canongate Books.

[7] Oettingen G. (2000). Expectancy Effects on Behaviour Depend on Self-Regulatory Thought: p101-129.

[8] Oates WJ (1940)The Stoic and Epicurean Philosophers, The Complete Extant Writings of Epicurus, Epictetus, Lucretius and Marcus Aurelius: Random House

[9] Antoninus MA (1742). Marcus Aurelius Antoninus. The Meditations of the Emperor Marcus Aurelius Antoninus [Internet]. Available from http://oil.libertyfund.org/titles/2133 (August 26, 2014).

[10] Ehrenreich B (2009). Bright-sided: How Positive Thinking is Undermining America: Metropolitan Books.

[11] Medina J (2009). Brain Rules: 12 Principles for Surviving and Thriving at Work, Home and School: Pear Press.

[12] Rossi E, Lippincott B (1992). The Wave Nature of Being: Ultradian Rhythms and Mind-body Communication [Internet]. Available from http://bit.ly/1zyCk4O (August 7, 2014).

[13] Barret R (2006). Building a Values-Drive Organization: A Whole-System Approach to Cultural Transformation: Butterworth-Heinemann.

[14] Alexander RJ (2005). Culture, dialogue and learning: Notes on an emerging pedagogy [Internet]. Available from http://bit.ly/1mN6Thb. (August 26, 2014).

[15] Lipman M (2003). Thinking in Education: Cambridge University Press.

[16] Fitzherbert A (1534). The Book of Husbandry. [Internet]. Available from http://bit.ly/YWjqK1 (August 26, 2014).

[17] Minsky ML (1986). Society of the Mind: Simon and Schuster.

[18] Bergland C (2011). No. 1 Reason Practice Makes Perfect [Internet]. Available from http://bit.ly/1q1lzwO (cited 26 August 2014).

[19] Goleman D (1996). Emotional Intelligence: Why It Can Matter More Than IQ: Bantam Books.

[20] Bandura, A (1977). Self-efficacy: Toward a unifying theory of behavioural change: Psychological Review, 84, p191-215. (1992) Exercise of personal agency through the self-efficacy mechanisms. In Schwarzer R (Ed.), Self-efficacy: Thought control of action, Washington, DC: Hemisphere. (1994) Self-

efficacy. In V.
S. Ramachaudran (Ed.), Encyclopedia of human behaviour, 4. New York: Academic Press, pp. 71-81.

[21] Hudson EM (2011). The Saboteur Within: Create Space Independent Publishing Platform.

[22] Abbott J, MacTaggart H (2009). Overschooled but Undereducated: Continuum Books.

[23] Forssén Ehrlin CJ (2014): The Rabbit Who Wants to Fall Asleep: A New Way of Getting Children to Sleep, North Charleston: Create Space.

[24] Hall LM, Belnap BP (2004). The Sourcebook of Magic: Crown House Publishing (p.118).

[25] Kuhn TS (1962). The Structure of Scientific Revolutions: University of Chicago Press [Internet]. Available
From http://bit.ly/1qrIAdB (cited 26 August 2014).

[26] Stone MH (1977). Healing the Mind: New York, WW Norton

[27] Einstein A, Infeld L (1966). The Evolution of Physics. Simon & Schuster, p.31.

[28] Lipman M (2003). Thinking in Education: Cambridge University Press.

[29] Willis J (2006). Research-Based Strategies to Ignite Student Learning: Insights from a neurologist/Classroom Teacher.

[30] Vygotsky LS (1967). Journal of Russian and East European Psychology, Volume 5, Number, 3 p.6-18.

[31] Medina J (2009). Brain Rules: 12 Principles for Surviving and Thriving at Work, Home and School: Pear Press.

[32] Piaget J (1928). La causalité chez L'Enfant: British Journal of Psychology, 18, p.276-301.

[33] Erickson MH, Rossi EL, Rossi SI (2010). Hypnotic Realities - The Induction of Clinical Hypnosis and Forms of Indirect Suggestion, Phoenix, Arizona: The Milton H. Erickson Foundation Press

[34] Izard CE, King KA, Trentacosta CJ, Morgan JK, Laurenceau JP, Krauthamer-Ewing ES, Finlon KJ (2008). Accelerating the development of emotion competence in Head Start children: Effects.

[35] Lipman M (1991). Thinking in Education, New York: Cambridge University Press.

[36] Bandler R, Grinder J (1975). The Structure of Magic, Vol. 1: Meta Press.

[37] Devore S (1981). Syber Vision Muscle Memory Programming for Every Sport and The Neuropsychology of Achievement Study Guide.

[38] Erickson MH, Rossi EL, Rossi SI (2010). Hypnotic Realities the Induction of Clinical Hypnosis and Forms of Indirect Suggestion, Vol 10, Phoenix Arizona: The Milton H. Erickson Foundation Press.

[39] Overdurf J, Silverthorn J (1996). Beyond Words: Languaging Change Through the Quantum Field. Audio-tapes.
PA: Neuro Energetics.

[40] De Bono E (2010). Six Thinking Hats, UK: Penguin.

[41] Zeigarnik BV (1927). Über das Behalten von erledigten und unerledigten Handlungen (The Retention of Completed and Uncompleted Activities), Psychologische Forschung, 9, p1-85.

[42] Bandler R, Grinder J (1975). Patterns of the hypnotic techniques of Milton H. Erickson, M.D, Cupertino: Meta
Publications & Erickson MH, Rossi EL, Rossi SI (2010). Hypnotic Realities the Induction of Clinical Hypnosis and Forms of Indirect Suggestion, Arizona: The Milton H. Erickson Foundation Press & Zeig JK (2003). The Language of Hypnosis A Phenomenological Approach. Available from: http://bit.ly/1tB2kN4 (cited 6th Aug 2014).

[43] Ofsted (2011). The last full inspection [Internet]. Available from http://bit.ly/1qrN3ge.

[44] Bodenhamer BG, Hall LM (1999). The User's Manual for the Brain, Volume 1, Wales: Crown House Publishing Limited. p232 & Owen, N (2001). The Magic of Metaphors, Wales: Crown House Publishing Limited & Gordon, D (1978). Therapeutic Metaphors, Capitola: Meta Publications.

[45] Satir V, Baldwin M (1983). Satir step by step: a guide to creating change in families, Palo Alto: Science and Behaviour Books.

[46] Satir V et al (1991). The Satir Model Family Therapy and Beyond, California: Science and Behaviour Books, p.121.

[47] Satir V et al (1991). The Satir Model Family Therapy and Beyond, California: Science and Behaviour Books, p.301.

[48] Hattie J (2011). Know thy impact, Visible Learning for Teachers, p5.

[49] Skinner, BF (1974). About Behaviourism, New York: Knopf.

[50] Gershoff, ET (2002). Corporal punishment by parents and associated child behaviour and experiences: A meta-analysis and theoretical review, p128, p539-579.

[51] Ask Dr. Sears [Internet]. Available from http://bit.ly/1onXMmX (cited 26 August 2014).

[52] Solter A (1992). The Disadvantages of Time-Out [Internet]. Available from http://bit.ly/1pEj4Sw (cited 26th Aug 2014).

[53] Dweck CS (2000). Self-theories: Their Role in Motivation, Personality and Development, Oxford: Taylor & Francis, p.2.

[54] Lipton BH (2007). The Biology of Belief: Unleashing the Power of Consciousness, Matter, & Miracles, California: Hay House p.93-94 & Mason, AA (1952). A Case of Congenital Ichthyosiform Erythrodermia of Broq Treated by Hypnosis: British Medical Journal 30, p.442-443.

[55] Cialdini, R (2007). Influence - The Psychology of Persuasion: Collins Business Essentials Ed edition

[56] Black P, Wiliam D (2006). Inside the Black Box: Granada Learning.

[57] Davis RB (1994). What mathematics should students learn, p.3-33.

[58] McGee PSUMO (2006). Shut Up, Move On: LifeCapstone Publishing (26 May 2006)

[59] Vygotsky LS (1986). Thought and Language, Cambridge, MA: MIT Press

[60] Bateson G (1972). Steps to an ecology of mind, San Francisco: Chandler Publishing Company

[61] Walker C (2006). Breathing In Blue [Internet]. Available from http://bit.ly/VMwFul (cited 17 November 2012).

[62] Dewey J, Hickman LA et al. The Essential Dewey, Vol. 2.

[63] Bodenhamer BG, Hall LM (1999). The User's Manual for the Brain, Wales: Crown House Publishing Limited. p232 & Overdurf J, Silverthorn J (1996). Beyond Words: Languaging Change Through the Quantum Field. Audiotapes. PA: Neuro Energetics.

[64] Satir V et al (1991). The Satir Model Family Therapy and Beyond, California: Science and Behaviour Books, p.62.

[65] Bandler R, Grinder J (1975). Patterns of the hypnotic techniques of Milton H. Erickson, M.D, Cupertino: Meta Publications, p.257-261 & Battino R, South TL (1999). Ericksonian Approaches A Comprehensive Manual. Wales: Crown House Publishing Limited, p.74 & Bodenhamer BG, Hall LM (1999). The User's Manual for the Brain Volume 1, Wales: Crown House Publishing Limited, p.149-150.

[66] Grinder JT, Bandler RW (1975). The Structure of Magic Palo Alto, CA: Science and Behaviour Books & Bandler LC (1985). Emprint Method: A Guide to Reproducing Competence.

[67] Charvet SR, Hall LM (2011). Innovations in NLP for Challenging Times.

[68] Rosen S (1991). My Voice Will Go with You, New York: W.W Norton & Company, p.222. & Charvet SR, Hall LM (2011). Innovations in NLP for Challenging Times.

16378272R00155

Printed in Great Britain
by Amazon